The Vegetarian Family

With recipes for a healthier life.

**By
Runa and Victor
Zurbel**

Edited by Lester Alexander

Prentice-Hall, Inc., Englewood Cliffs, N.J.

Printed in the United States of America
Prentice-Hall International, Inc., London
Prentice-Hall of Australia, Pty. Ltd., Sydney
Prentice-Hall of Canada, Ltd., Toronto
Prentice-Hall of India Private Ltd., New Delhi
Prentice-Hall of Japan, Inc., Tokyo
Prentice-Hall of Southeast Asia Pte. Ltd., Singapore
Whitehall Books Limited, Wellington, New Zealand
10 9 8 7 6

Library of Congress Cataloging in Publication Data
Zurbel, Runa
      The vegetarian family.

      Bibliography: p.
      Includes index.
      1. Vegetarian cookery.   I. Zurbel, Victor,
joint author.   II. Alexander, Lester.
III. Title.
TX837.Z87   641.5'636   78-5238
ISBN 0-13-941468-1
ISBN 0-13-941476-2 pbk.

This book is dedicated to Swami Satchidananda,
who passed on to us the wisdom of the vegetarian way of life,
as well as so many other wonderful gifts.

CONTENTS

Introduction *1*

The Vegetarian Family's Basic Training *5*

1 Where Do Elephants Get Their Protein? *9*

2 Cooking Vegetables Without Killing Them *13*

3 Whole Grains for the Whole Family *33*

4 Beans Can Fill Up More Than Bean Bags *61*

5 From Hamburgers to Soyburgers *77*

6 Macrobiotics: East Meets West *83*

7 Tofu: The Food of the Future – Discovered
    Over Two Thousand Years ago *89*

8 "Open Sesame" The Magic of Seeds and
    Nuts *103*

9 Sauce as a Source of Nutrition *117*

10 Say "Cheese," But Not Too Often *121*

11 Let Us Be Fruitful *129*

12 Juices Keep Our Juices Flowing *139*

13 Snacks Can Be Healthful *145*

14 Born Free and Natural *153*

15 How to Use Your Kitchen
    Cabinet as a Medicine Cabinet *161*

16 Food for Thought *167*

    Bibliography *176*

    Index *180*

    Photo Credits *185*

Introduction

The purpose of this book is not to convert you to vegetarianism. Rather, it will introduce you to delicious, natural, whole foods and allow you to discover for yourself how the addition of these foods to your diet can be a healthful and joyful experience—as it has been for us.

It will also introduce you to the concept that the human body has the ability to go through life in a state of health and well-being, free from illness and disease, when it is nourished with natural, whole, unrefined foods without additives such as preservatives, sugar, and artificial ingredients. And that when the body does fall ill, it also has the remarkable ability to heal itself, with the assistance of herbs, foods, and natural healing techniques.

We have been vegetarians for ten years and our two boys, Oliver (age 7) and Jonathan (age 4) have been vegetarians since birth.

We became vegetarians after an introduction to yoga and after an extraordinary journey around the world exposed us to a variety of delicious and nutritious foods that we had never known existed.

As meat eaters, all we knew of vegetarian foods were the limp vegetables that were served as side dishes to our sirloin steak or roast beef, and the salads consisting of iceberg lettuce and tomatoes. After experiencing the taste of delightful vegetarian foods in Hawaii, Japan, Hong Kong, Thailand, Malaysia, India, Ceylon, the Mid-East, and Europe, we had another picture entirely. Eating vegetarian foods was so natural after this trip that we became vegetarians automatically. Now, rather than thinking of ourselves as vegetarians, we think of ourselves simply as people who eat foods that are biologically and ecologically suitable—most of which happen to be vegetarian.

There are books on vegetarianism which maintain that, although man required meat at times for survival, we are biologically constructed as vegetarian animals. And it has been demonstrated that the consumption of large quantities of meat leads to a degeneration of health, contributing to various ailments and diseases such as arthritis and rheumatism, gallstones and kidney stones, respiratory diseases, heart disease, and even cancer.

All the hormone, pesticide, and other toxic residue found in meat is another good reason to look at the alternative of eating high-protein vegetarian foods. Also, cattle consume 14 to 21 times more protein than they yield. Eating vegetarian foods, we have the satisfaction of knowing that we are contributing to our own health and well-being as well as to that of the starving mass of people on our planet.

We could cite numerous other reasons for eating vegetarian foods—moral, spiritual, and psychological—but the one we will accent here is simply that the foods we will introduce you to are delicious and healthful.

We have collected hundreds of delectable vegetarian recipes and have included our favorites; but more important in this book are the basic methods of preparation and cooking that can make anyone an excellent chef of vegetarian cuisine.

We want you to be able to walk into a health food store

and know what to look for—to be able to recognize millet from cous-cous, to know the difference between short-grain and long-grain rice, to know what tofu, tahini, and tamari are. Then, we want you to know how to store the foods and how to prepare them in the easiest and most convenient way.

Many of the books we have read about vegetarian cooking are written by people living a leisurely life with lots of time to prepare their food. Consequently, these books have elaborate, time consuming recipes. As working parents with two active children, we just don't have a lot of time to spend preparing a meal. Our goal, therefore, is to prepare meals that combine optimum nutrition and taste appeal with a minimum amount of time and effort. We would rather spend our time making homemade tofu or whole-grain bread than we would preparing an exotic recipe for an evening's meal. The bread and tofu will last for many meals, whereas the exotic meal is going to be enjoyed just once.

Whole foods cookery is an entirely different concept of cooking from standard cookery. Although it *can* be a culinary art, there is a great joy and satisfaction that comes from the whole, natural taste of the food itself, and it doesn't really require more than some basic simple cooking techniques to bring it to its peak of taste and nutritional potential.

We hope that this book will get you to think for yourself about the foods that are best for you and will enable you to discover your own abilities and creativity in preparing satisfying vegetarian meals, without having to rely on this or any other book. We sincerely wish that you enjoy yourself as much as we did while discovering the wonderful world of vegetarian foods.

Runa and Victor Zurbel

The Vegetarian Family's Basic Training

UTENSILS

We use pots of stainless steel, baked enamel over cast iron, and carbon steel (like the wok). We threw out all of our aluminum pots years ago, as aluminum seems to impart an unpleasant flavor to natural food and many negative qualities have been attributed to the toxic residue that aluminum leaves behind. We also avoid plastic, especially for any food or liquid that is hot, as the heat may release the vinyl chlorides in the plastic.

Among the utensils we keep in our kitchen are several saucepans (stainless steel or baked enamel), a large and a small frying pan (baked enamel), several large pots (baked enamel over cast iron), a stainless steel pressure cooker, two stainless steel steamer baskets, a large and a small wok, a large colander, strainers, an onion chopper, a chopper-grater, a garlic press, a cast iron pancake pan, and a clay teapot.

Our electrical appliances include a blender, a juice extractor, an electric coffee grinder (for grinding nuts and seeds), and a toaster-oven, which is very convenient for broiler sandwiches, roasting nuts and seeds, toasting muffins and baking small casseroles.

The foods that make up our list of basics are those we use often and always keep in stock; whenever we make a dish that requires an infrequently used ingredient, we buy the amount we intend to use at that time. We buy most of our staples in bulk and store reserves in our basement in large glass jars that we get from restaurants or restaurant supply stores. We keep a working supply of these basics on the kitchen shelf in large glass apothecary and mason jars.

Most of the recipes in this book call for ingredients from our list of basics, with the occasional additions of other foods and spices. Please note that as we are firmly against the use of sugar, none is included in any of the recipes. Eggs are included in some recipes, and those who are strict vegetarians may wish to try the recipe without the eggs.

Basic Grains

Brown rice (long grain or short grain)	Oats
	Cous-cous
Millet	Bulghur wheat
Kasha (buckwheat groats)	

Flour

Whole wheat flour (stone-ground preferred)	Soy flour
	Wheat germ
Cornmeal	Bran
Arrowroot flour	

Beans

Soybeans	Garbanzos
Lentils	

Seeds

Sesame	Pumpkin
Sunflower	

Seeds for Sprouting

Alfalfa

Mung beans

Nuts

Almonds (Raw)

Cashews (Raw)

Nut Butters

Peanut butter

Almond butter

Tahini (sesame butter)

Oils (unrefined, cold-pressed)

Safflower or sunflower

Sesame

All-blend

Corn or peanut oil

Olive oil

Seasonings and spices

Tamari sauce (naturally
    fermented soy sauce)

Spike or vegetable salt (available
    in most health food stores)

Miso (fermented soybean paste)

Kelp, granulated

Sea salt

A variety of herbs

Supplements

Brewer's yeast

Protein powder (Shaklee or
    other brand)

Sweeteners

Honey (raw, uncooked)

Fructose (fruit sugar)

Blackstrap molasses
    (unsulphured)

Date sugar

Pure maple syrup

Teas

Peppermint

Camomile

Spearmint

Rosehip

Chapter 1

Where Do Elephants Get Their Protein?

Quite often when people discover that we are raising our children as vegetarians, they ask the question: "Where do they get their protein?" To which, we usually answer with another question: "Where do elephants get *their* protein?"

The elephant, which is the strongest beast in the animal kingdom, builds up the protein in its body from the amino acids in the vegetation it eats, as the wild horse builds up its magnificent body from the grass it eats. Likewise, the human being has the ability to build up protein from amino acids present in the vegetable kingdom.

When man eats meat, he is, in effect, getting the amino acids second hand. The animal ate the vegetation to build up its protein. And in order for man's body to utilize the animal protein, it must be broken down to its original amino acid structure. Carnivorous animals are too highly toxic for the human body, and this is the reason the meat man eats comes from vegetarian animals.

Why not go right to the beginning of the food chain and get protein first hand from nature? Nature supplies abundant protein in nuts, seeds, beans, grains, and vegetables. Vegetarian proteins may be lower in gram value than meat protein, but they are more easily assimilated.

We Americans have been brainwashed into thinking that we need huge amounts of animal protein, when in fact it has recently been discovered that an overabundance of animal protein can be detrimental to health and has been linked to the causes of many diseases.

One of the world's leading nutritionists, Dr. Paavo Airola, states that the proteins in vegetables, fruits, and many seeds and nuts are biologically superior to animal proteins, and that it is virtually impossible not to get enough protein in your diet provided you have enough to eat of natural, unrefined foods. His real concern is that Americans are not getting enough vitamins and minerals in their foods.

We have two beautiful boys, and we attribute much of their health, strength, and awareness to their natural vegetarian diet. Ironically, when we are asked the question about "enough protein," it often comes from a mother whose children look like they themselves need protein.

Actually it's not protein the children need, but fresh, raw or properly cooked vegetables and whole, unrefined foods. We seldom see other children eating fresh vegetables that are raw, or at least not overcooked, whereas our sons Oliver and Jonathan can often be seen munching on an organic carrot.

In our family we ensure that all of our protein requirements will be met by including in our diets whole grains and beans, fresh sprouts and vegetables, nuts and seeds, tofu, miso, and tamari, and occasional dairy products and eggs.

The manner in which foods are prepared and combined also has a great deal to do with the amount of protein obtained from them. In the following chapters we will discuss how to combine foods for added protein value and share with you our many delicious recipes for easy-to-prepare, high-protein dishes.

Perhaps you too will discover, as many people have, that the human body has the potential for constructing high-quality protein from the amino acids that are available in the food that nature provides and that you can be as strong as a beast without having to eat one.

Chapter 2

Cooking Vegetables Without Killing Them

The first lesson we give in our vegetarian cooking course is how to cut and cook a carrot.

Vegetables are an important part of your diet, a major source of vitamins and minerals, but it you prepare vegetables the way most Americans do, you probably might just as well eat junk food.

Many vitamins are water-soluble. If vegetables are boiled in a lot of water and then the water is poured down the drain, much of the nutrition goes with it. What's left on the plate is lifeless and tasteless; that's why it usually remains on the plate.

As a child I never liked cooked carrots. Now they are among my favorite vegetables. When Runa and I have guests for dinner, we enjoy serving carrots and always get an enthusiastic response to them. People say: "These carrots are delicious! What did you do to them?" What we did to them was let them be carrots. First we cut them not in dull round slices, but Japanese style—long, diagonal slices. Then we steam them (the right amount of time and not a minute longer) and then serve them (with nothing more than a little tamari sauce and sesame seeds, letting the real taste come from the carrot itself and not the seasoning). Of course, having fresh, organically grown carrots can make a big difference in taste.

Unfortunately, in most American kitchens, in both homes and restaurants, vegetables are overcooked, depleted of their vitamins, and then disguised by pouring on thick sauces, glazing with honey, or adding mounds of butter.

What a difference when one eats fresh broccoli or string beans, gently steamed "al dente" (to the tooth) rather than limp and pale from overboiling in water. Oliver and Jonathan absolutely refuse to eat overcooked vegetables, but finish up every one when they are tenderly steamed. Is it any wonder so many children dislike vegetables, considering the way they have been served to them?

SELECTING VEGETABLES

Vegetables that are in season are usually priced lower. Nature provides the proper foods for the proper season and one shouldn't have to rely heavily on frozen or freighted produce shipped from one climate to another. Although a little deviation doesn't hurt, one should learn to live according to one's climate.

Select vegetables that have the deepest and brightest color and are unblemished. Have you ever noticed carrots that are displayed in plastic bags with orange stripes to make them look more orange? Organically grown vegetables do not have to go through this deception.

Contrary to the way most people shop, we do not always

14

reach for the larger vegetables. When Runa first came to America from Sweden, she was as amazed by the size of the vegetables as she was by the size of the automobiles. The fruits and vegetables Runa was brought up on in Sweden were miniatures compared to those in America, but they more than made up for their size in taste and in vitamin and mineral content.

The Modern Farmer.

In the early 1900's people in Sweden received postcards such as these from their relatives who had emigrated to America.

15

COOKING VEGETABLES

Steaming

An essential utensil to have in your kitchen is a stainless steel steamer basket. Steaming is the easiest and one of the most nutritious methods of cooking vegetables.

Using a pot with a tight lid, put in just enough water so that it falls short of touching the bottom of the steamer basket. Salt the vegetables lightly if you prefer (with sea salt), and steam them until they are just tender or "al dente." The color is at its brightest at this point and then rapidly starts to lose its brilliance. Since stoves and pots vary, you'll have to watch carefully at first and determine for yourself the proper cooking times. Certain vegetables that take the same amount of cooking time can be effectively combined in the same pot.

Serve immediately with butter, soy margarine, tamari, or fresh lemon juice and topped with sesame seeds or gomasio (sesame salt—recipe given in Chapter 8).

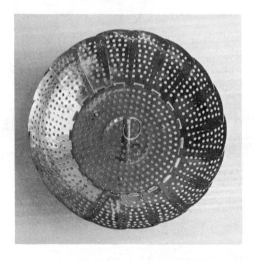

Vegetables with Arrowroot

Our friend Eve showed us another tasty and simple way to cook vegetables while preserving the water-soluble vitamins. She cooks them in a large pot with a little water. Just before they are fully cooked, she adds arrowroot flour and tamari sauce or miso, turning the stock into a delicious gravy. To add arrowroot to the vegetable pot, first dissolve a tablespoon of the flour in about ¼ cup of water. Add to the vegetables a minute or two before they are done.

Arrowroot flour is a nutritious, high-mineral food that can be used in place of cornstarch or flour to thicken gravy, soups, fruits, etc. It is made from the roots of a tropical American plant. You can also use kudzu, which is considered superior in quality to arrowroot and is an extract of the kudzu root, noted for its medicinal value.

Wok Cooking

The word *wok* means cooking vessel. In fact, it's probably one of the oldest cooking vessels known to man, and certainly one of the most versatile. Its uses in Chinese as well as Western cooking are almost unlimited. It can be used for deep frying, sautéing, and steaming. The shape and composition of the wok allow for an efficiency and speed of cooking that is almost impossible to improve upon.

Woks come in various sizes and metals. We prefer the traditional carbon steel wok. The wok will look brassy when you first use it, but time will blacken it to distinction.

After the wok has been seasoned, all you have to do to clean it after cooking is to rinse it with hot water and scrub it with a nylon brush or scouring pad. Detergent is not necessary, and should even be avoided.

How to Season a Wok

1. Wash wok with soap and hot water. Rinse and dry carefully.
2. Coat the inside surface with a light film of oil (preferably peanut oil).
3. Heat the wok over high heat for a minute. Rinse with hot water.
4. Oil and heat the wok again, rinse with hot water, and dry over heat.
5. The wok is ready to use.

Stir-Fried Vegetables

One of the advantages of stir-frying vegetables in a wok is that it is a quick and efficient method of cooking a wide variety of vegetables in the same dish. Another advantage is that the oil locks the vitamins in. And the third is that it is delicious.

Grouping Vegetables for Wok Cooking

Vegetables are cut to expose the maximum surface to heat and grouped according to their cooking times, as indicated below. Those taking the longest time to cook are added first (Group A) followed by the other groups.

Group A: broccoli, cauliflower, carrots, string beans, asparagus, celery, turnips

Group B: onions, green peppers, snow peas, cabbage, potatoes, Chinese mushrooms

Group C: bean sprouts, lettuce, spinach, celery cabbage, tomatoes, mushrooms, cucumber, bamboo shoots, water chestnuts

Group D: squash, eggplant, tofu

Add two or three tablespoons of oil to wok (a preferred oil to use is peanut oil as it smokes only at extremely high temperatures; we also use a combination of soy and sesame oil). Add a clove of minced or whole garlic and a small piece of whole or grated fresh ginger root. Heat over medium flame (if whole clove garlic and ginger root is used, sizzle in oil until the oil is flavored and then discard).

Add about ½ teaspoon sea salt and stir in Group A. Stir vegetables until the color begins to change, becoming brighter and translucent, then spread them along the side of the wok and add Group B. Stir until color changes, then spread them along the side and add Group C, followed by Group D.

You may also add a little water while cooking, and, just before the vegetables are done, thicken with a tablespoon of Arrowroot flour dissolved in ¼ cup of water, stirring the mixture into the vegetables.

Easy Chinese Wok Dinner

3 Tbs. vegetable oil
1 clove minced garlic
1 slice fresh grated ginger
2 cups frozen or fresh peas
6 to 8 Chinese mushrooms, presoaked, or 1 cup sliced
    fresh mushrooms
1 cup diced tofu (optional)
1 cup mung or soybean sprouts

Heat oil in wok with garlic and ginger. Add peas and mushrooms and stir for a few minutes. Add tofu and stir in for a few minutes more. Add sprouts and stir.

Serve with brown rice and Tahini Sauce (see Chapter 9).

Easy Indian Wok Dinner
Curried Peas and Cauliflower

4 Tbs. oil
1 large onion, finely chopped
1/4 tsp. tumeric
1 tsp. cayenne
1 tsp. ground cumin
1 tsp. sea salt
1 cup peas, frozen or fresh
1 cup cauliflower, chopped small

Saute onion in oil in wok. Add spices and stir. Add peas and cauliflower and stir well. Cover and cook over low flame for about 10 to 15 minutes or until vegetables are tender.

Serve with brown rice and beans (or tofu), or with brown rice and Onion Tahini Sauce (see Chapter 9).

Nituke Vegetables

This is the Japanese method of stir-frying in which the vegetables are cut into matchstick pieces and stir-fried in very little oil. The cooking is quicker than with larger-cut vegetables.

Slice root vegetables diagonally very thin (preferably, with a Japanese vegetable knife), then slice the diagonal pieces into matchstick size pieces. Vegetables like broccoli and cauliflower can be cut up so the flowerettes look like miniature trees, and the stalks can be diced small or cut into matchstick pieces.

Once you have the vegetables cut, heat a tablespoon of peanut, or sesame and soy oil. Put the vegetables in the wok or pan and stir constantly, cooking 5 to 10 minutes over a high flame. Reduce to a medium flame and cook 10 to 15 minutes longer, stirring constantly. A few minutes before it's done, add tamari sauce and a tiny bit of water.

Tempura Vegetables

Tempura is a traditionally Japanese method of deep frying with a batter. In India it's known as pakura. You can tempura almost every vegetable, even parsley and spinach leaves.

We use a combination of oils for tempura; corn, sunflower, and sesame oil. We keep it in a quart bottle in the refrigerator, labeled "tempura oil," and reuse it for several batches.

Cut and prepare vegetables as you do for nituke and place them in refrigerator to cool while you prepare the batter.

Tempura Batter

You can vary this batter by mixing other flours such as buckwheat with unbleached white, buckwheat with rice flour or chick-pea flour, or in combination with whole wheat flour. We have also enjoyed using just chick-pea flour.

1 cup whole wheat flour

1 to 1¼ cups cold water

½ tsp. sea salt

1 egg (optional)

The batter must be kept cool. For best results use ice cold water.

For frying tempura, use about 3 inches of oil heated to 350 degrees or a little higher. The right amount of heat can be critical, so it would be best to use a frying thermometer.

When the oil reaches 350°, dip the vegetables into the batter (preferably using chopsticks, as your fingers will warm it up), and then gently drop them into the oil. The temperature will drop as soon as you add the vegetables but will soon come up again. Vegetables are left in for a few minutes depending upon their size. The time varies so much that you'll have to use your own judgement. Then remove the vegetables and leave them to drain while adding more to the pot.

Be careful not to overheat the oil. If it starts smoking with no food in it, turn off the heat and gently drop in a raw onion to cool it off. Try to keep your oil as free of excess bits of batter as possible.

It is hard to tell how much batter is needed for the amount of vegetables you intend to use. You will be surprised how much it takes, so prepare more than enough at first. You can always throw clumps of leftover batter in by the spoonful for miniature popovers.

We serve tempura with small individual bowls of Ginger Tamari Sauce (see Chapter 9).

Indian Vegetarian Cookery

We love Indian food and have lived on quite a variety of it on our travels through India. Indian cookery, however, is very time-consuming and requires a good deal of attention. And since we live near New York City where there are dozens of Indian restaurants, we don't often cook it at home.

Making curry properly requires several hours of preparation and cooking. We have time only for our half-hour curry, which is quite good, incidentally.

Vegetable Curry

4 Tbs. oil
2 tsp. mustard seed
2 tsp. tumeric
1 tsp. coriander seed
1 tsp. cayenne
2 tsp. cumin seed
1 tsp. sea salt
1 cup carrots, diced
2 cups string beans, cut
1 cup peas, fresh or frozen
1 cup potatoes, diced
2 cups water
½ cup yogurt

Heat oil in large pot. Add mustard seed until it dances; add remaining spices and salt, then stir. Add vegetables. Stir again and add water. Bring to a boil, add yogurt, stir, and simmer for 20 minutes.

Upma

Upma is not one of our "whole food" recipes, as one of the main ingredients is cream of wheat. We also use frozen vegetables. But it is a delicious treat and can be prepared to serve a large group of people. We were first introduced to it at a yoga retreat where it was prepared for hundreds of people. There are many variations, but this one is our favorite.

1/2 cup vegetable oil
1/2 cup slivered or cut almonds
1 tsp. mustard seed
2 tsp. sea salt
1 Tbs. curry powder
1/4 tsp. chili powder
1 tsp. ground cumin
1 tsp. coriander
1 tsp. caraway seeds
2 cups frozen mixed vegetables
2 cups water
1/2 cup raisins (optional)
1 cup cream of wheat

Slightly sauté almonds in oil with mustard seed. Watch that the almonds don't burn. Add salt and other spices. Add vegetables. Stir and sauté for a few minutes. Add water. Let it come to a boil and simmer under cover for 10 minutes. Add raisins, if desired. Add cream of wheat, stirring constantly as you add. Simmer, covered, for about 5 minutes.

Serve with yogurt or sour cream. Apple sauce on the side is nice also. Upma tastes great the next day, too, cold or heated up.

Vegetable Casseroles

We usually prepare our vegetable casseroles with a simple grain dish, on the side or included in the recipe. We have found casseroles ideal for dinner guests; we prepare them earlier and put them in the oven to cook, or reheat if previously cooked, just before the guests arrive.

Vegetable casseroles that include beans and grains, or cheese, constitute a complete meal and are a simple delight to serve. If you're lucky enough to have any left over, it makes an easy lunch the next day.

Below is our recipe for a delicious rice, cheese, and vegetable casserole. You'll find more casserole recipes in Chapters 3 and 4, on grains and beans.

Vegetable Casserole with Cheese

2 cups cooked brown rice
2 cups broccoli, cut
2 carrots, cut in julienne strips
1 zucchini, sliced
1 cup green beans, cut
1 16-ounce jar marinara sauce
1 cup (4 ounces) shredded Monterey Jack
   or cheddar cheese (or combine half of each)
¼ cup sesame seeds

Preheat oven to 375°. Place rice in bottom of casserole dish. Steam vegetables for 5 to 7 minutes, then spoon vegetables over rice. Top with marinara sauce. Cover and bake for 30 minutes. Sprinkle cheese over casserole and top with sesame seeds. Return to oven uncovered, to melt cheese (about 5 minutes). Season to taste at table.

We usually don't bake vegetables during the summer months because the oven heats up the kitchen. When winter comes, however, we bake winter squash, potatoes, and sweet potatoes.

Honey Squash

3 medium acorn squash
¼ cup melted butter or margarine
¼ tsp. cinnamon
½ tsp. sea salt
¼ tsp. ginger
⅓ cup honey

Preheat oven to 375°.

Cut squash in half lengthwise. Remove seeds and stringy fiber. Place cut side down in shallow baking pan and surround with ½ inch hot water. Bake 30 minutes.

Combine remaining ingredients. Pour off liquid from pan and turn squash cut side up. Pour honey sauce into hollow of squash and bake 15 minutes, basting with sauce occasionally.

Vegetarian Chopped Liver

1 pound fresh string beans
3 Tbs. oil
2 large onions, finely chopped
1 stalk celery, finely chopped
¼ cup chopped walnuts
3 hard-boiled eggs
sea salt, to taste

Steam string beans until barely tender. Heat oil in skillet and sauté onions until tender. Add celery and cook 2 minutes longer. Chop or put in meat grinder: string beans, onion mixture, walnuts, and eggs. Season with salt and/or tamari. Put in refrigerator to chill before serving.

Vegetable Soup

We are generally a one-course family and don't prepare soups as part of a meal. The soups we do make are usually thick and rich and are a meal unto themselves.

Our vegetable soup can be considered as either a soup or a stew, depending upon how much water is used. It always comes out slightly different and we usually make it with whatever leftover vegetables we have on hand.

Chop up available vegetables, such as carrots, broccoli, string beans, peas, potatoes, celery, spinach leaves, dulse, seaweed, etc. Heat ¼ cup of vegetable oil in a large pot, and a chopped onion. Then add the vegetables. Season with tamari sauce, miso, or sea salt. For added flavor and body you can add vegetable bouillon cubes, Vege Base, or herbs such as bay leaves or dill.

Add as much water as you prefer. Less water will make it come out as a stew. More water will make it a soup. Cook for 20 to 25 minutes. To thicken it you can add millet, cous-cous, or whole wheat noodles and cook along with the soup.

Dr. D'Adamo's Soup

This simple and nutritious soup recipe comes from our naturopathic doctor. It is presented here without spices, but you can add garlic, tarragon, thyme, rosemary, basil, and sea salt, seasoning to your own taste.

Base for soup:

1 potato, diced

1 large carrot, diced

5 stalks of celery, cut up

Boil above ingredients in 4 cups water (3 cups, if you like it thicker) for 10 minutes; liquify with the water in a blender. You now have a creamy soup base. Add sliced carrots, string beans, diced potatoes, celery, and parsley; simmer over low heat until vegetables are tender. Add some water, if necessary.

Vegetable Broth

We take any vegetables we have at hand and chop them up in every conceivable way, since we use only the broth and discard the vegetables. You can follow this outline and use any vegetables, unpeeled, but thoroughly washed.

potatoes, unpeeled, cut in cubes
carrots, coarsely chopped
celery, chopped
squash, chopped
green beans, cut in half
mushrooms, cut, stem and all
onions, chopped
greens: spinach, watercress, parsley, cabbage
sea salt or tamari to taste

Cover vegetables with water and cook until done. Strain broth and season with sea salt or tamari; discard vegetables.

RAW VEGETABLE SALADS

Raw vegetables are alive with enzymes, which do get destroyed when vegetables are cooked. Therefore it is advisable to include a serving of raw vegetables in your daily diet. The quality of the vegetables really makes the quality of the salad. The first and foremost thing we do in preparing a salad is to find vegetables of quality, preferably organic or home grown.

We usually prefer very simple salads, such as a variety of different lettuces, sprinkled with snips of fresh basil leaves and tossed with an Italian-style herb dressing.

Raw vegetables such as broccoli, cauliflower, zucchini, and others that are usually cooked should also be included, chopped up small, in salads. We often arrange a plate of fresh, raw vegetables and serve it with a dip.

Raw carrots, cabbage, beets, and apples are enjoyable and easy to eat, especially for children, when they are shredded.

Below are a few sample salad recipes that we have enjoyed.

Carrot and Raisin Salad

6 cups grated carrots
1 cup raisins
Combine and serve with lemon juice, lemon juice and honey, or oil and apple cider vinegar.

Variation
Add grated apples, and/or grated zucchini.

Greek Salad

3 cups raw spinach or lettuce (or combine)
2 tomatoes, quartered
1 cup fresh, black pitted olives
1 pound crumbled or diced feta cheese
3 stalks celery, diced

Combine all ingredients in a bowl and serve with lemon juice or your favorite dressing.

Spinach Salad with Sesame Seed Dressing

1 pound spinach leaves
1 cup sunflower seeds or 1 cup chopped walnuts
1 bunch parsley, chopped fine
½ cup safflower oil
½ cup lemon juice
1 Tbs. honey
4 Tbs. sesame seeds
¼ tsp. cayenne
½ tsp. sea salt

Combine spinach leaves with seeds or nuts and parsley. Blend remaining ingredients until smooth and pour over salad as desired.

Guacamole

2 ripe avocados
1 small onion, grated
3 Tbs. lemon juice
½ tsp. kelp powder
½ tsp. chili powder
2 Tbs. ketchup (optional)
¼ cup mayonnaise

Mash the peeled avocados in a bowl with a fork until smooth. Season with onion, lemon juice, kelp, chili powder, and catsup, if desired. Mix well. Adjust seasoning to taste.

Form mixture into a mound and cover with a layer of mayonnaise to keep it from becoming dark; refrigerate, covered, until ready to serve. Just before serving, stir the mayonnaise into the mixture. Serve with taco chips.

Chapter 3

Whole Grains for the Whole Family

Whole grains are one of the most important parts of our vegetarian diet. They are one of our main sources of protein and contain nearly all the B vitamins, vitamin E, unsaturated fats, and numerous other vitamins and minerals. Refining removes a large percentage of these nutrients, and despite the claim that refined foods are "enriched," they are only partially enriched with synthetic vitamins. Because all nutrients are interdependent, refining throws off the whole nutritional balance, rendering them useless, in our opinion. Adelle Davis compared the labeling of "enriched" with the example of the highway robber who takes your car and your money and then gives you back some change to take the bus home.

BREADS

When Oliver and Jonathan were smaller, and we used to walk past the bread section in the supermarket, they would sometimes ask for a loaf of white bread to feed to the ducks. That's the association our children have with white bread—it's food for the ducks. They would never think of eating it themselves, not after having been brought up on Runa's homemade whole-grain bread.

33

As sorry as we feel for the ducks, we feel even sorrier to see other children eating white bread. If their parents tried the following simple experiment, they might think twice before giving their children refined, bleached, and preserved flour products. Take off the crusts from about four slices of white bread, then tightly knead a ball out of the remaining part. Now just imagine a ball like that sitting inside your digestive tract, or your child's.

Naturopathic doctors tell us that many diseases are caused as a result of the digestive organs being clogged up with white flour and other refined food products.

There is a television commercial that shows people squeezing a loaf of white bread as a demonstration of its freshness. The squeezing demonstration may prove something for toilet paper, but it doesn't prove a thing to us about the benefit of eating the white bread. Eat enough of that squeezable, doughy white bread, however, and you may end up saving money on toilet paper, because you'll be constipated.

If you have any white bread in your house now, we recommend taking the children to the park and letting them feed the ducks with it. And if you have any bleached white flour in the house, don't throw it away. Here is a recipe for making homemade play dough.

Play Dough

1 tsp. artificial food coloring
1 cup tap water
2½ cups white refined, bleached flour
1 cup common table salt

Put coloring in water. Mix all ingredients together. Knead until it's a good consistency. Add more flour if it's too sticky. Invite children to help.

We could go on about the valuelessness of white bread and its many detriments to health, but we prefer to accentuate the positive and encourage you to bake your own whole wheat bread. Once you get a taste of the real thing, you'll never want to go back to the other.

When we bake bread, we like to get Oliver and Jonathan involved. They help by adding the ingredients, kneading the dough, and shaping their own little loaves. How proud they are when they take them out of the oven! If you have children, get them involved when you bake bread. In addition to providing them with a lot of fun, it is a wonderful education to learn what elements go into the food that goes into their bodies.

Honey Whole Wheat Bread

Our many thanks to the Integral Yoga Institute for the original recipe, to which we have made some slight modifications. This has become our basic bread recipe and we vary it by varying the flours.

¾ cup honey (use less or none, if you prefer)
3 cups hot water
3 Tbs. fresh or packaged yeast
1 Tbs. salt
¼ cup safflower oil
9 cups whole wheat flour (approx.)
oil for bowl
butter for pans and brushing tops of loaves

Pour honey into hot water and mix. When water is lukewarm, dissolve yeast in water. Add salt and oil to mixture, stirring after each additional ingredient.

Pour 5 cups of flour into water and combine well. Add 2 more cups of flour and mix. Add rest of flour slowly, controlling the consistency of the dough so that it is moist and flexible. The dough must be workable and not stick to the bowl.

Knead dough at least 10 minutes. For effective kneading, fold one side at a time toward the other systematically, then press down heavily on the dough with heels of palms.

After kneading, turn dough into an oiled bowl with the smooth side facing down. Then roll dough over so it remains in bowl with smooth surface on top. Cover with damp cloth and let dough rise in a *warm* place (like top of gas stove) for an hour or until it doubles in size.

Punch dough down, pressing out the gas. Return to warm place and let rise again for 45 minutes. Punch down again and turn dough onto flat surface. Cut dough carefully with knife. Shape loaves, forming smooth tops, and place in pans greased with butter. Let rise for 20 minutes or until dough rises to tops of pans. Makes 2 to 3 loaves, depending on size.

Bake in preheated 350° oven for 40 to 60 minutes. After loaves have begun to brown (about ½ hour) brush tops with melted butter. Bread is done when thumping of the top produces a hollow sound, and when bottom is firm.

Variations

Substitute ½ cup of soy flour or corn flour for ½ cup whole wheat flour.

Substitute ½ cup corn flour, ½ cup soya flour, and ½ cup wheat germ for 1½ cups whole wheat flour.

Substitute 2 cups unbleached white flour for 2 cups whole wheat.

Mix in a few handfuls of raisins, nuts, chopped dates.

Once you have baked our bread, try our herb toast.

Herb Toast

½ cup melted butter or soy margarine

¼ tsp. each: chives, basil, thyme, marjoram

Melt butter and add herbs. Let stand for at least a half hour. Reheat and dip in slices of whole wheat bread. Place in moderately heated oven for about 20 minutes.

Add minced garlic for Garlic Herb Toast.

There are also many delicious quick breads, muffins, cookies, and pancakes that you can quickly and easily make from whole grains. The recipes are simple and foolproof. Once you've tried these recipes, you may want to improvise on them by adding skim milk powder, brewer's yeast, wheat germ, soya powder, lecithin, sprouts, and other nutritional supplements.

Yogurt Bran Muffins

1 cup whole wheat flour
1 cup bran flakes, or ½ cup bran flakes plus ½ cup wheat germ
½ tsp. sea salt
3 tsp. baking powder (aluminum-free)
1 cup yogurt
1 egg
¼ cup honey or maple syrup
3 Tbs. oil
½ cup raisins or chopped dates
Preheat oven to 425°.

Combine and mix together dry ingredients. In separate bowl beat together yogurt, egg, honey, and oil. Add dry ingredients to yogurt mixture and mix only enough to moisten. Fold in raisins or dates.

Fill cups of oiled muffin pan ⅔ full and bake 15 to 20 minutes or until done.

Carrot Cornbread

1¼ cups cornmeal
1 cup grated carrots
1 or 2 Tbs. honey or maple syrup
3 Tbs. oil
1 tsp. sea salt
1 cup boiling water
2 eggs, separated
Preheat oven to 400°.

Combine first five ingredients, then pour boiling water over them. Beat egg yolks and add to mixture. Fold in stiffly beaten egg whites. Pour batter into well-buttered 9-inch square pan. Bake for 30 minutes or until firm.

Early American Cornbread

1 egg
1 cup milk
2 Tbs. maple syrup or honey
1 cup cornmeal
¾ cup wheat flour
2½ tsp. baking powder (aluminum-free)
1 tsp. salt
3 Tbs. oil
Preheat oven to 425°.

Beat egg lightly. Add milk and maple syrup. Mix together the dry ingredients and sift into the liquid. Add oil, and stir briskly. Pour in 8 by 8 inch greased pan and bake for 20 minutes. Or pour into an oiled muffin pan for corn muffins.

Cornmeal and Rye Muffins

1 cup cornmeal
1 cup rye flour
2 Tbs. wheat germ
2 tsp. baking powder (aluminum-free)
¾ tsp. sea salt
2 tsp. honey
2 eggs, well beaten
1 cup skim milk
4 Tbs. oil
Preheat oven to 425°.

Mix dry ingredients together. Combine honey, eggs, milk, and oil. Add to dry ingredients, stirring until moist. Spoon mixture into oiled muffin pan and bake for 20 minutes or until firm.

Easy Rye Bread

Even if you don't usually like rye bread, you'll find this bread delicious. And it is so easy to make.

2 cups rye flour
1/2 tsp. salt
2 tsp. baking powder (aluminum-free)
1/2 cup skim milk powder
1 cup milk
2 Tbs. oil
1 Tbs. honey or maple syrup (optional)

Preheat oven to 450°.

Combine dry ingredients. Stir together milk, oil, and honey (if desired), then stir into dry mixture until smooth. Oil and flour a cookie sheet. Place dough on the sheet, flour your hands, and form dough into circle or square 1/2 inch thick. Prick dough with fork several times and bake until lightly browned, about 10 minutes.

Sesame Whole Wheat Crackers

1 cup whole wheat flour
3 Tbs. sesame seeds
1/2 tsp. sea salt
1 or more cups cold water

Preheat oven to 350°.

Mix flour, 2 tablespoons sesame seeds, and sea salt in bowl. Gradually add water while stirring. Batter should be a little loose, but can be lumpy. Drop batter by spoonfuls onto an oiled cookie sheet. Sprinkle remaining sesame seeds on top and bake for 30 minutes.

Whole Wheat Bread Sticks

2 cups whole wheat flour
1¼ cups milk
½ cup safflower oil
2 cups wheat germ
1 Tbs. honey
sesame seeds, as needed
Preheat oven to 350°.

    Combine all ingredients except sesame seeds, and knead until smooth. Cut dough and roll into sticks, ¼ to ½ inches thick and about 5 inches long. Roll in raw sesame seeds, place on oiled cookie sheet, and bake for 45 minutes or until brown.

Banana Bread

2 cups whole wheat pastry flour
½ tsp. sea salt
½ cup maple syrup
⅓ cup vegetable oil
4 eggs, separated
¼ cup milk
3 ripe mashed bananas
½ cup chopped walnuts
Preheat oven to 350°.

    Mix flour and salt. Add maple syrup and oil. Beat in egg yolks and mix well. Add milk, mashed bananas, and chopped nuts. Beat egg whites and fold in. Turn into medium-size oiled loaf pan, and bake for 50 minutes.

Whole-Grain Pancakes

This is not the typical American pancake. But perhaps it should be! One of our whole-grain pancakes is far superior in nutrition to a whole stack of those doughy roadside-diner pancakes.

Once you familiarize yourself with the basic recipe, adapt it to your own taste and add your own ingredients such as brewer's yeast, protein powder, lecithin, bran, wheat germ, etc.

1½ cups whole wheat flour
3 tsp. baking powder (aluminum-free)
1 tsp. salt
2 Tbs. maple syrup or 1 Tbs. fructose (optional)
2 cups milk (or 1 cup milk, 1 cup water)
1 or 2 eggs, slightly beaten
3 Tbs. oil (safflower preferred)

Combine dry ingredients. Combine liquid ingredients and stir into dry ingredients until moist. If mixture is too thick, add water or milk. If too thin, add flour. Heat skillet with a thin covering of oil or butter. Spoon pancake batter onto hot skillet. When bubbles appear on surface, turn and brown other side.

Serve with maple syrup, honey, fructose (sprinkled on top), apple sauce, or apple butter. Or for a different approach try tahini and tamari sauce; this is an interesting way of serving pancakes for dinner, by the way, with steamed vegetables on the side.

Variations

Mix flours. Examples: 1 cup whole wheat flour and ½ cup corn
    flour.
Or ¾ cups whole wheat flour, ½ cup corn flour, ¼ cup soy flour.
Add a few tablespoons of high-protein powder or soy flour. Com-
    pensate by adding more liquid or less whole wheat flour.
Substitute ½ cup of oatmeal for ½ cup of flour.

Waffles may be made from the same ingredients, increasing the oil to ⅓ cup and using 2 eggs.

Pita (Flat Bread)

2 cups water
3 Tbs. oil
1 tsp. yeast, diluted in ½ cup lukewarm water
6 cups whole wheat pastry flour
1 Tbs. salt

Mix water, oil, and diluted yeast in bowl. Gradually blend in flour and salt. Knead on slightly floured board for 5 minutes until smooth and elastic. Place in bowl, oil top, cover bowl, and set in warm place to rise overnight.

The next morning knead for 3 minutes more and then shape into 3-inch balls. Flatten each ball with hand and roll out on board to a 7- or 8-inch circle. Place on an oiled baking sheet and let stand 1 hour. Bake in preheated 350° oven for 20 to 25 minutes.

To use, make slit, cut off end, or cut and put filling in pocket.

Whole Wheat Scones

2 cups whole wheat flour, or 1 cup whole wheat flour plus 1 cup
    unbleached white flour plus 1 Tbs. wheat germ
3 tsp. baking powder (aluminum-free)
1 tsp. sea salt
⅓ cup butter or oil
1 cup milk (skim or whole)

Preheat oven to 450°.

Mix flour with baking powder and salt. Mix in butter or oil. Add milk and mix. Drop large spoonfuls of dough onto lightly oiled cookie sheet. Bake 10 minutes. Makes 12 to 14 scones.

Serve with any of the following: butter; honey; apple butter; strawberry, apricot, or rose hip jam.

There are also many delicious and nutritional breads that you can buy from your grocer or supermarket or at a health food store. Many of the leading companies now offer health breads and sprouted wheat and rye breads.

The health food store breads are still far superior in taste and nutrition to the supermarket breads, but there is one kind of bread found in the supermarket that we recommend most heartily—the crisp Scandinavian rye breads. They come flat, in cracker form, and are available in many variations such as thin or thick, light or dark rye, and with or without caraway seeds. Some popular brands are Wasa Brod, Rye King, Finn Crisp, and Ideal Flatbrod. If you are lucky, you may find the large, round flats. Runa's mother sends us these breads from Sweden occasionally and are they delicious!

These breads are made with nothing but whole-grain flour, salt, and water. In Sweden, they often have them with cheese and thin slices of cucumber on top. There were no corn flakes in Sweden when Runa grew up, so she used to crumble up pieces of this *knackebrod* in a bowl, pour milk or buttermilk over it, and put fresh lingenberries (similar to cranberries) on top.

COUS-COUS

Children love to eat cous-cous as much as they like to say it. It was one of the first words out of Jonathan's mouth. We can still remember his sweet little lips pucker as he sat at the dinner table and said very distinctly, "coos-coos." It is a hand-processed kind of wheat cereal from Northern Africa (Tunisia, Algeria, and Morocco). Although it is not truly a whole grain, it is an excellent cereal for children, because it is light and easy to digest. You will enjoy it yourself, especially since it is one of the easiest grains to cook.

Basic Cous-Cous

1 cup cous-cous
¼ tsp. salt
2 cups boiling water
1 Tbs. butter

To boiling water in saucepan, add cous-cous and salt. Boil gently for about 2 minutes. Turn off flame, add butter, cover, and let stand for 10 minutes.

Peppers Stuffed with Cous-Cous

The recipe for this delightful, fresh-smelling, and easy-to digest dish was borrowed from the Integral Yoga Institute. We hope you enjoy it. Try it for lunch. This recipe makes a dozen stuffed pepper halves.

6 green peppers
2 cups cous-cous
4 cups water
3 to 4 Tbs. butter
3 to 4 chopped tomatoes
1 bunch chopped scallions
salt to taste
12 small slices cheese (cheddar works nicely)
6 tsp. sesame seeds

Wash and halve green peppers lengthwise, removing veins and seeds. Steam lightly and set aside.

Cook cous-cous in water for 2 or 3 minutes; let stand for 10 minutes, then add butter, chopped tomatoes and chopped green scallions.

Mix well, salt to taste. Stuff cous-cous mixture in pepper halves. Cover each pepper with a slice of cheese, sprinkle sesame seeds on top, and place in warm oven until cheese melts.

BROWN RICE

Whole brown rice is a storehouse of nutrition. It is the best balanced of all the grains and is the main staple of the macrobiotic diet system. White rice, like white flour, has been stripped of its most valuable components, thus being made a high-starch, carbohydrate food with little of the protein, calcium, phosphorus, iron, or B-complex vitamins left. We eat white rice only on rare occasions, such as when eating out in a Chinese or Indian restaurant. We look forward to the day when these restaurants also include brown rice in their menus.

Brown rice does, however, require more work to digest than white rice; that is why the macrobiotic diet recommends chewing each mouthful fifty times. Even if you don't manage to chew it that much, you can be conscious of chewing it until it is fully masticated.

We Americans tend to gulp everything down fast. Chewing, however, is a very important process for us to be aware of. It affects the entire digestive system, the salivary glands, the colon, intestine, etc. Make a game out of chewing with the children. See who can chew the longest. Give them the opportunity to learn what Mahatma Gandhi said about eating: "You should drink your foods and eat your liquids."

Brown rice, or any whole grain, for that matter, is suitable for children who have their full set of teeth. In many countries of the world, mothers chew the brown rice and other grains first and then serve them to their infants. Brown rice can be put in a blender after cooking for easier digestibility, or even better, it can be ground down to a fine "cream of brown rice" flour before cooking.

You should cook brown rice regularly, always making a generous amount; it keeps well in the refrigerator and can be sautéed or added to various dishes the following day. A brown rice product that is available in health food stores and in some supermarkets is "rice cakes." They are round, puffed cakes of brown rice and children love them as much as popcorn. Serve them plain, with butter, or with peanut butter. They are especially good with tahini and honey. Oliver loves to take rice cakes along with his school lunch.

Buy only *organically grown* brown rice, as commercial rice is one of the most heavily chemicalized food crops.

Basic Brown Rice

1 cup brown rice
2 cups water
1/4 tsp. sea salt

Wash rice thoroughly in strainer. Put rice and water in pot and bring to a boil. Lower flame and simmer for 45 minutes to 1 hour or until water is absorbed and the bottom of the rice is slightly scorched. (The scorched part is considered desirable in macrobiotic diets because it is the most "Yang" and richest in minerals. In many traditional Japanese families, scorched rice was first offered to the sick and elderly.)

Variations

Dry-roast rice in pan before cooking for a more nutlike taste and aroma.

Prepare as above, adding 1 teaspoon tamari sauce to the water for each cup of rice.

Prepare as above, adding 1 tablespoon roasted sesame seeds to each cup of rice for Sesame Rice.

Pressure-Cooked Brown Rice

1 cup brown rice
1½ cups water

Prepare as above. Cook over low flame at 15 pounds of pressure, for 40 minutes. Let pressure return to normal. This doesn't take much less time than the regular way, but you may enjoy it more.

Sweet Brown Rice

Prepare as for Basic Brown Rice. Halfway through the cooking add a mixture of raisins, chopped dates and chopped nuts (about a cup), stirring into the rice and continue cooking. Sprinkle cinnamon on top when done. For added sweetness add a little maple syrup.

Fried Rice with Almonds

½ onion
3 scallions
½ stalk celery (optional)
3 Tbs. sesame oil
2 cups cooked brown rice
1 Tbs. tamari sauce
⅓ cup slivered almonds

Chop onion, scallions (reserving part for garnish), and celery and saute in sesame oil. Add brown rice and stir-fry. Season with gomasio (sesame salt), tahini, or tamari sauce. Garnish with almonds and some chopped green scallions.

Variation
Add 2 tablespoons sesame seeds while stir-frying.

Brown Rice Soup

Here's a delicious soup you can make with precooked brown rice and beans. It makes an easy complete meal.

1 onion, sliced
1 cup sliced carrots
1 cup green beans, cut
2 or 3 Tbs. oil
3 to 4 cups water
1 tsp. sea salt
1 cup cooked brown rice
1 cup cooked beans
2 Tbs. miso

Saute onion, carrots, and green beans in oil. Add water and salt. Bring to a boil, lower flame. Add cooked rice and cooked beans and simmer until vegetables are tender—about 20 minutes. Add miso to a little stock from the pot, mix and add to pot. Let stand for 10 minutes before serving.

Cream of Brown Rice

1 cup brown rice
4 cups water
pinch of sea salt

Wash brown rice thoroughly, drain well, and toast in dry skillet until dry, about 5 minutes. In nut mill or coffee mill, grind to a powder. Return rice powder to dry skillet and toast lightly.

Bring water, with a pinch of salt, to boiling point. Gradually sprinkle in ground rice so that water doesn't cease to boil. Reduce heat and boil gently for about 15 minutes.

Variations

May also be cooked with milk or a combination of milk and water.
Sweeten with honey, molasses, date sugar, or maple syrup.
Cook with chopped raisins, dates, or figs.
Cook with sliced apple and sprinkle with nutmeg and cinnamon.

MILLET

Millet is considered to be the king of grains. It has been a staple food for as far back as records exist in Northern China and Northern India. Millet is eaten by the Hunzas, the people of the Himalayas who play volleyball at the age of 90. This is a hearty grain that is high in protein, minerals, and vitamins and can provide both adult and child with a lot of energy. The seed of the millet contains four times as much fluorine as barley, corn, oats, rye, or wheat. In India and Africa, bread made from millet is an important part of a pregnant woman's diet, since it is believed to help the development of the infant's bones, cartilages, tendons, and teeth.

Basic Millet

1 cup millet
1 tsp. oil
4 cups boiling water
¼ tsp. sea salt

Sauté millet in pot with oil, stirring constantly, until it turns slightly brown. (You'll love the nutlike aroma. It smells a little like fresh popcorn.) Add boiling water and salt. Cover, lower flame, and let simmer for 20 to 30 minutes.

Serve with butter, Whole Wheat Sauce (see Chapter 9), or tamari. Or serve sweetened with honey for breakfast.

Millet and Vegetables

1 cup millet
2 tsp. sesame or corn oil
2 cups chopped vegetables
3 cups boiling water
½ tsp. sea salt

Dry-roast millet in pot until slightly browned. In a pan, sauté vegetables in oil. Combine millet and vegetables, add water and salt, and simmer in covered pot or bake in covered casserole at 350° for 30 to 40 minutes.

Millet Casserole

1 cup millet
4 cups water
2 tsp. sea salt
2 onions, chopped
1 clove garlic, finely chopped
2 cups tomato puree
1½ cups wheat germ
2 Tbs. oil
2 tsp. dry sweet basil (2 Tbs. if fresh)
2 Tbs. chopped parsley
½ tsp. celery seeds
1 Tbs. tamari

Place millet, water, and salt in saucepan. Bring to a boil, cover and simmer for 30 minutes.

Preheat oven to 350°. Add remaining ingredients to millet and turn into oiled casserole dish. Bake for 1 hour.

Variation

15 minutes before done, add grated cheese topped with 2 tablespoons raw sesame seeds and return to oven.

KASHA (BUCKWHEAT GROATS)

Unlike most grains, buckwheat is actually the fruit rather than the seed of the plant. It is commonly found in Russia and Eastern Europe, where people often have it for breakfast. It has lots of protein, is high in B vitamins, and, because it produces body heat, it can keep you going for quite a while, as many Russian athletes would testify.

We have never tried it for breakfast, but we do love it with dinner. It has a beautiful brown color, which we complement with the orange of carrots and the deep green of string beans or broccoli. Kasha is easy to prepare and can be cooked in about twenty minutes.

Basic Kasha

1 cup buckwheat groats
1 Tbs. corn oil
2 cups boiling water
1/4 tsp. sea salt

Sauté kasha in pot with oil until the groats darken. Add boiling water and turn down flame. Add salt, cover, and simmer for about 15 minutes. Add salt and/or tamari to taste.

This dish is delicious with many sauces. We like it with Whole Wheat Sauce or Tahini Sauce (see Chapter 9), or just eat it plain. It also goes well with yogurt or sour cream.

Variation

First saute a chopped onion and green pepper in 2 tablespoons oil. Then add kasha, stir, and saute until it turns darker. Add boiling water and salt, cover, and simmer for 15 minutes.

OATMEAL

Oatmeal is one of the finest foods there are for growing children. It contains all the bran, middlings, endosperm, and germ portion natural to the grain, and unlike other whole grains it can be bought in almost every grocery store. Oatmeal is one of the richest silicon carriers known and as such is ideal for children to prevent infection from many contagious diseases. It is also very high in phosphorus, potassium, and magnesium, minerals which are important for the formation of brain and nerve elements. Oatmeal water is extremely beneficial to infants as well as sick patients. We generally use oatmeal in the most common way, as porridge, but also add it to breads, cookies, and lentil loaves.

Oatmeal Date Blend

Cook oatmeal according to instructions on box, adding chopped dates before you cook. After oatmeal is cooked, put in blender with a little milk or Soy Milk (see Chapter 4), and blend until smooth and creamy. Delicious for babies!

Variation

For Cinnamon-Raisin Oatmeal, cook as directed, adding raisins and cinnamon before cooking.

Homemade Granola

If you've never made your own granola, don't buy another package until you bake it for yourself. There is no comparison in freshness and flavor. And it fills your home with the most delicious aroma. We make it using whatever appropriate ingredients we have at hand, but to get you started, here is our basic recipe with variations listed below.

4 cups rolled oats (old-fashioned)
$\frac{1}{2}$ cup wheat germ
$\frac{1}{4}$ cup chopped almonds
$\frac{1}{4}$ cup chopped cashews
$\frac{1}{4}$ cup pumpkin seeds
$\frac{1}{4}$ cup sesame seeds
$\frac{1}{4}$ cup sunflower seeds
$\frac{1}{2}$ cup raisins
$\frac{1}{4}$ cup honey
$\frac{1}{4}$ cup oil
$\frac{1}{4}$ tsp. vanilla extract (optional)
Preheat oven to 325°.

Combine oats, wheat germ, nuts, seeds, and raisins. Heat together honey, oil, and vanilla extract. Pour over mixture and mix well to coat all ingredients evenly. Spread onto one large or two smaller shallow baking pans.

Bake for 20 minutes or until lightly browned. Stir after first 10 minutes so ingredients at bottom have a chance to brown. Baking time varies, so check to see raisins don't burn.

Cool and store. Serve in individual portions with milk, buttermilk, or Soy Milk (see Chapter 4).

Here are some ingredients that you can use for variations: bran flakes, coconut, soy flakes, filberts, walnuts, peanuts, rye flakes, currants, dates.

Maple Almond Granola

Here's another granola recipe which you can freely improvise upon by adding other nuts and seeds.

2 cups oat flakes
1 cup almonds, coarsely chopped
¼ cup maple syrup
⅓ cup corn oil
¼ tsp. salt
½ tsp. vanilla extract
Preheat oven to 350°.

Mix all ingredients together and spread thinly on a cookie sheet. Bake 20 minutes or until lightly browned. Stir halfway through baking.

Muesli

This is a version of the cereal they serve and have made famous at a Swiss health spa.

1 Tbs. oatmeal, soaked overnight in ⅓ cup water
2 Tbs. ground almonds
1 Tbs. lemon juice
1 Tbs. honey
2 apples, grated
¼ cup chopped almonds

Combine soaked oatmeal, ground almonds, lemon juice, and honey, and mix well. Mix in grated apples. Serve sprinkled with chopped almonds.

Naturally Sweet Three-Grain Breakfast Cereal

½ cup rolled oats
½ cup millet
½ cup buckwheat groats
½ cup finely chopped sunflower seeds
1 cup raisins, chopped dates, or dried prunes
½ cup dried apples (optional)

Put all ingredients to soak in cold water to cover overnight. In the morning, bring to a boil over moderate heat, adding more water if needed. Serve with milk, Cashew Milk (see Chapter 8), or Soy Milk (see Chapter 4). Needs no sweetening.

BARLEY

Barley is one of our oldest known cereal foods, cultivated over 2,000 years before Christ and known in ancient China, Egypt, Greece, and Rome. It is high in mineral salts and contains a lot of iron. An Indian Doctor of Herbal Remedies recommended barley water as a good drink for babies because it builds up the hemoglobin.

Barley thickens the water or stock it is cooked in, so it is an excellent ingredient for thick, rich soups.

Barley Water (Good for babies)

¼ cup barley
2 quarts water
2 Tbs. dark honey or molasses (optional)
few drops of lemon juice (optional)

Place barley in pot with water. Bring to a boil and simmer for about 45 minutes, stirring occasionally. Strain water into quart bottle. Use as is or add dark honey or molasses and a few drops of lemon juice.

Save barley for breakfast. Heat it up with a little milk and maple syrup, and sprinkle wheat germ on top. Blend smooth for baby.

Mushroom Barley Soup

Mushroom Barley Soup is a standard in all the established vegetarian and dairy restaurants.

1 Tbs. oil
2 onions, chopped
1 stalk celery, sliced thin
1 cup sliced mushrooms
1 cup barley
5 cups water
1 bay leaf
1 Tbs. sea salt
¼ tsp. pepper

In pot, sauté onions, celery, and mushrooms in oil for 5 minutes. Add barley and sauté with the vegetables for 5 minutes more. Add water and bring to a boil. Add bay leaf, salt, and pepper, and cook covered over low heat for about an hour.

For richer, creamier soup substitute a cup of milk for a cup of water. Or you may substitute a cup of Cashew Milk (see Chapter 8) or Soy Milk (see Chapter 4).

BULGHUR WHEAT

Bulghur is a precooked cracked wheat, with the wheat germ and bran intact. Because it is cracked and precooked, it can be prepared in a matter of minutes. It is used mainly in the traditional dishes of Wheat Pilaf and Tabouleh Salad, but we always keep it on hand because it is a main ingredient in one of our favorite casserole dishes (see Mediterranean Soybean Casserole in Chapter 4).

Tabouleh

2 cups cracked wheat or bulghur
1 cup warm water
1 cup chopped parsley
1 medium onion, finely chopped
2 tomatoes, chopped
2 Tbs. fresh mint (or 1 tsp. ground dried mint, or 1 tsp. thyme)
juice of 2 lemons
½ cup unrefined oil
sea salt and pepper to taste

Soak the cracked wheat in warm water for 1 hour. Add the other ingredients and toss lightly. Refrigerate before serving. If you like it tangier, add more lemon juice. Some prefer it with more oil as well.

SUMMARY

There is such a wide variety of grains and such a great number of things that can be done with them that anyone who asks us vegetarians what we eat is generally in for a big surprise. And we haven't even gotten to beans yet!

Before we end our discussion of whole grains, just a few words on how to store them. We have found it best to store our grains in large glass jars. We can see just what we have, and can keep insects out at the same time. Once we really got into our vegetarian way of life, we pulled down a whole wall of kitchen cabinets and replaced them with shelves of large bottles where we store all our staples in full view. We are proud to display our wonderful foods to guests. A lineup of large glass jars filled with whole grains is truly a sight to behold. And a diet of them is even better!

Chapter 4

Beans Can Fill Up More Than Bean Bags

If you travel around the world, you'll see that in most traditional cultures grains and beans are eaten together. In Mexico, corn tacos and tortillas are eaten with pinto beans. The peasants of Cuba eat rice with black beans. In India, chappati (flat unleavened bread) are eaten with dal (lentils or peas). In China and Japan, tofu (bean curd) is eaten together with rice.

Instinct tells our bodies to seek protein by combining grains and beans, and scientific evidence now supports what natives of the land have known for thousands of years—that grains and beans complement each other. Together, they supply the amino acids that build protein in the human body. When eaten together, they not only provide a complete source of protein but increase their combined protein value by as much as 20 percent. The book *Diet for a Small Planet* by Frances Moore Lappe discusses this concept in detail and provides some excellent recipes for grain and bean dishes.

There are as many varieties of beans as there are grains, and countless ways to prepare and serve them. We are continuously learning about and exploring new ways to serve beans. We have encouraged our children to learn about beans by allowing them to play with them. Oliver and Jonathan have spent many a quiet hour seated in the middle of the kitchen floor playing with a bowl of beans while we prepared dinner. We've found no toy that can compete with beans, a strainer, funnel, cups, measuring spoons, and other kitchen utensils as a source of concentrated play for the young child. It really adds to their experience to play with the same soy, aduki, or pinto beans that wind up on their dinner plate a short time later.

We store our beans as we do our grains—in large glass jars in a cool, dark room in the basement. We keep our daily supply of beans in glass apothecary jars on our open shelf in the kitchen.

Following are descriptions of the beans we most frequently use and our favorite recipes. We also on occasion use kidney, navy, lima, and black beans as well as peas.

SOYBEANS

Soybeans are one of the most versatile foods for meatless cooking, one of the few legumes that contain a complete protein. And quite a lot of protein it is: twice as much as meat and fish, twice as much as cheese, and four times as much as eggs.

For thousands of years soybeans have been the "meat" of the Orient and have been used in countless variations. Tofu, or bean curd, as it is sometimes called, is available in many different forms and textures. It is only recently that soybeans have become popular in the West, and every indication is that they will be one of our greatest sources of protein in the future as more and more people turn away from high meat consumption.

It is said that the soybean production of Kansas, Nebraska, and the Dakotas alone could feed the entire population of the United States. As more people turn toward this vegetarian protein, the agricultural cycle of our planet will become more efficient and the end of starvation will become a reality.

In addition to the enormous variety of delicious soybean casseroles and other dishes, soybeans can be made into milk, curd, sprouts, soup, and flour to enhance the food value of breads. You can also make roasted soybeans, or buy soybean nuts, which are roasted, hulled, split soybeans. They are excellent for lunch box snacks or as party food.

Our very favorite soybean dishes are tofu and tempeh. Tofu is a soybean product that is made by curdling soybean milk, draining off the fat, and compressing the curds into a cheeselike form. Tempeh is made by fermentation. We think these two dishes are so delicious and such a major source of protein for the future that we have devoted an entire chapter (Chapter 7) to them.

For this chapter, we are offering you our favorite soybean dishes and casseroles, along with basic instructions for soybean preparation.

Basic Soybeans

One cup of dry soybeans makes 3 cups of cooked beans. Place desired amount in bowl, cover with water, and let stand overnight. Drain, rinse, and cover with 4 cups of fresh water for each cup of dried beans. Bring to a boil in covered pot, lower heat, and simmer for about 2½ hours. Just as they get tender, add ½ tsp. sea salt for every cup of soybeans.

For more flavor, you may also add to the pot the following ingredients per cup of soybeans: 1 small onion, diced; 1 bay leaf; 1 tablespoon oil; 1 tablespoon chopped celery.

Mediterranean Soybean Casserole

½ cup dried soybeans
1 cup bulghur wheat
1 cup boiling water
2 Tbs. oil
1 onion, finely chopped
1 green pepper, finely chopped
salt and pepper to taste
½ tsp. Tabasco sauce
2 Tbs. chopped parsley
1 pound feta cheese, crumbled
1 can tomatoes (1 lb., 14 oz.)
1 tsp. ground cumin

Soak soybeans overnight in water to cover. Next day, drain and place beans in electric blender. Add 1 cup fresh water and blend until smooth.

Preheat oven to 375°. Pour 1 cup boiling water over bulghur and set aside.

Heat oil in skillet and sauté onion and green pepper until tender. Add soybean mixture, then bulghur after it has absorbed all the water. Then add salt, pepper, Tabasco, and parsley.

Spread half the mixture in bottom of an oiled 3-quart casserole and sprinkle on half the cheese. Combine the tomatoes and cumin and spoon half over the cheese. Repeat layers with the remaining ingredients: mixture, cheese, then tomatoes. Cover and bake 1 hour; remove the cover and bake for another 15 minutes.

Yield: 6 to 8 servings. Keep leftover in refrigerator and enjoy for lunch or dinner, cold with salad or heated up.

Soybean Casserole

3 Tbs. vegetable oil
1 medium onion, chopped
1 clove garlic, chopped
½ green pepper, chopped
3 cups cooked soybeans
½ cup tomato sauce
1 tsp. sea salt
½ cup bread crumbs
4 ounces cheddar cheese, grated
3 Tbs. sesame seeds
Preheat oven to 375°.

Heat oil in large skillet. Sauté onion, garlic, and green pepper. Add soybeans, tomato sauce, salt, and bread crumbs, and mix. Transfer mixture into an oiled casserole dish. Sprinkle cheese on top, and then sesame seeds.

Cover and bake for 20 minutes or until cheese is melted.

Soybean Salad

1 can or 1 cup cooked soybeans
mayonnaise to taste
1 stalk celery, finely chopped
1 tsp. celery seed
Spike, Vegesalt, or sea salt to taste

Mix all ingredients and serve on salad platter. Or mash and serve on sandwiches like tuna salad. Add grated carrots if you like. Or add alfalfa sprouts for a chewy salad.

Also try Chick-Pea Salad, replacing soybeans with chick-peas in the above recipe.

Soy Milk

1 cup soy flour
4 cups water

Mix water and soy flour. Let stand at room temperature for a couple of hours. As it sticks easily, cook soy milk in a double boiler for about 45 minutes. Or cook in a large pot, stirring constantly. For a smoother soy milk, strain through cheesecloth.

Pour into quart jar and cool in refrigerator.

Hints

A chopped vanilla bean added while cooking gives a good flavor.

A tablespoon of lecithin added to the quart bottle will help keep it in suspension.

Variation

Sweeten with a tablespoon of honey, if you like.

May also be sweetened with molasses, maple syrup, or fruit syrups, and flavored with carob powder.

Or, add fresh fruit such as bananas or blueberries, and blend until smooth.

Sesame Soy Milk

This formula takes advantage of all the nutrients of soy milk, complemented by the high calcium content of the sesame seed. And since soy and sesame are complementary proteins, their combination yields an abundance of high-quality protein, making it ideal for babies, growing children, and nursing mothers.

1 cup Soy Milk, warm (see preceding recipe)
1 to 2 Tbs. tahini
honey or molasses to taste

Combine all ingredients and mix well.

Roasted Soybeans

1 cup dry soybeans
4 cups cold water
sea salt to taste

Soak soybeans in water overnight.

Preheat oven to 200°. Drain water and dry the beans. Spread beans in shallow pan and bake for 2 hours, turning them over occasionally. Salt to taste.

Follow same directions to make Roasted Chick-peas.

GARBANZOS (Chick-Peas)

Garbanzos, when combined with whole wheat, other whole grains, or sesame seeds, provide a good source of protein. By themselves, however, they do not contain all the essential amino acids that make up a complete protein.

They have a delicious nutlike flavor, and we use them mostly in the Mid-East dishes of hummus and felafel or cold in salads. Our children also eat them cold as finger snacks.

Hummus is a Mid-East dish that is served as a dip, along with the flat whole wheat bread called pita. You tear off a piece of pita and scoop up the hummus. This dip can be served at parties along with chips and raw vegetable sticks; or simply serve it as a salad on a bed of lettuce.

Felafel are fritters made of chick-peas and other ingredients, deep-fried and then served in the pockets of pita bread with some salad and tahini poured over the top.

We can give you the recipes of the hummus and felafel we had while we were in Israel, but unfortunately we cannot provide you with the atmosphere in which we discovered them sitting in outdoor cafes in Jerusalem and other places in the Biblical land.

Hummus

2 cups chick-peas, canned or cooked (cook as Basic Soybeans, in this chapter)
1 to 2 cloves garlic, minced
2 Tbs. tahini
1/2 tsp. olive oil
juice of 1/2 lemon
sea salt to taste
paprika
parsley

Puree cooked chick-peas and mix together all ingredients, except paprika and parsley, until smooth and creamy. Serve in a bowl, with paprika sprinkled on top and garnished with parsley. Use as a dip for vegetables or pita bread.

Felafel

1 cup cooked chick-peas, or 1 15-ounce can chick-peas
2 Tbs. whole wheat flour
2 Tbs. chopped parsley
1/2 tsp. baking soda
1/2 tsp. sea salt
1 clove garlic, minced
dash cayenne
oil for deep fry

Mash chick-peas well. Stir in remaining ingredients, except oil. Flour hands and shape mixture into 1-inch balls.

Heat oil in frying pan or wok. When oil is hot (test with small piece) fry chick-pea balls for about 2 minutes or until they are golden brown, turning once. Drain on paper towels.

Serve in whole wheat pita bread with lettuce and Tahini Sauce (see Chapter 9), or serve as appetizers or hors d'oervres with Tahini Sauce or Yogurt Roquefort Sauce (see Chapter 10).

LENTILS

Lentils are one of the oldest of mankind's foods. They are the quickest to prepare of any of the legumes: they cook in less than 45 minutes and do not need presoaking.

The lentil, like most of the other legumes, is not a complete protein by itself and needs to be combined with a whole grain. In India, we tasted quite a variety of lentils, usually served with chappati or rice. We use lentils in soup, lentil burgers, lentil loaves, and combined with rice.

Basic Lentils

1 cup lentils, washed
2 cups water
¾ tsp. salt
2 bay leaves
optional (one or more):
¼ cup chopped onion
¼ cup chopped green pepper
¼ cup chopped or sliced celery
1 clove garlic, minced
½ tsp. cumin, ground

Combine all ingredients in pot and cook, covered, over medium heat for about 30 minutes or until lentils are tender.

Lentil Soup

1½ cups lentils
1½ quarts water
½ tsp. sea salt
2 stalks celery and tops, chopped
1 onion, sliced
2 carrots, diced
2 Tbs. oil
1 Tbs. lemon juice
1 tsp. tarragon

Put lentils in pot. Add water and sea salt. Cover and simmer until almost tender. Add all other ingredients. Cover and simmer until carrots are done, about 15 minutes longer.

Variations

Add tamari or vegetable bouillon cubes.
For a thicker soup, puree cooked lentils and return to soup.

Curried Lentils with Rice

3 large onions, chopped
½ cup vegetable oil
1 cup lentils
1 cup brown rice
6 to 7 cups water
1 Tbs. sea salt
1½ tsp. curry powder
minced parsley, to garnish

Cook onions slowly in oil until soft and golden, and set aside. Meanwhile cook lentils and rice in water for 35 minutes. Add salt, curry powder, and onions. Cook another 20 minutes or until most of water is absorbed. Garnish with minced parsley.

This tastes great cold, too.

Lentil Salad

2 cups cooked and drained lentils
3 Tbs. apple cider vinegar
2 Tbs. olive oil
1 tsp. sea salt
1 onion, finely chopped
1 stalk celery, finely chopped

Marinate lentils overnight in vinegar, oil, and salt mixture. Combine with other ingredients and chill thoroughly. Serve over salad greens.

Lentil Loaf

2 medium onions, chopped
2 medium tomatoes, diced
1 Tbs. oil
2 cups lentils, cooked
1 cup bread crumbs (part of which can be wheat germ)
1 Tbs. parmesan cheese, grated
½ cup milk
¼ tsp. garlic powder
1 tsp. salt
1 egg
Wheat germ for sprinkling

Preheat oven to 350°.

Sauté onions and tomatoes in oil. In bowl, mash lentils. Add onions and tomatoes. Mix in all but the last ingredient. Spoon mixture into oiled loaf pan. Sprinkle wheat germ over top. Bake for 30 minutes

Variations

Sprinkle grated cheese and sesame seeds on top 10 minutes before done.
Try it with cheese on top covered with tomato sauce.

ADUKI BEANS

The aduki bean is a small red bean that is much used in macrobiotic cooking. It is high in protein and is supposed to be very good for ailing kidneys. It is also said to be the only alkaline and non-gas-forming bean.

Aduki Beans

Soak beans overnight. Drain and add 4 cups of water for each cup of soaked beans. Cook for 3 hours or until beans are soft.

In pressure cooker: Add 2½ cups water for each cup of soaked beans. Cook for 45 minutes. Add salt and/or tamari to taste.

Aduki Bean Soup

1 cup cooked aduki beans
4 cups water
1 Tbs. oil
1 medium onion
1 carrot, grated
1 tsp. basil

Add beans to water in pot and bring to boil. Meanwhile sauté onion, carrot, and basil in oil. Add to pot and cook for 20 minutes.

OTHER BEAN RECIPES

Vegetarian Chili

3 Tbs. oil
2 cloves garlic, finely chopped
2 onions, chopped
2 Tbs. chili powder
$\frac{1}{4}$ tsp. cayenne pepper
2 tsp. sea salt
1 tsp. granulated kelp
2 tsp. oregano
2 Tbs. tamari
4 tomatoes, diced
4 cups cooked kidney or pinto beans

In large saucepan sauté garlic and onions in oil. Sprinkle in chili powder, cayenne pepper and sea salt and cook for a minute. Add the next four ingredients, cover, and simmer for about 20 minutes. Add water if it gets too dry. Mix in beans and let stand covered for 10 minutes. Reheat if necessary.

Serve with Early American Cornbread (see Chapter 3), brown rice, or tacos. If there is any left over the next day, you can mash it, refry it, and serve in tortillas with shredded lettuce and grated Monterey Jack cheese.

Black Bean Soup

This hearty, smooth soup is a tradition in the Orient. Maybe it will be in your home too.

1 cup black beans
4 cups water
2 Tbs. oil
2 onions, chopped
1 stalk celery, sliced
½ tsp. sea salt
1 bay leaf
1 tsp. celery seed
¼ tsp. basil
juice of ½ lemon
1 to 2 Tbs. tamari
1 Tbs. arrowroot (if needed)

Soak beans overnight in water.

Sauté onions and celery in oil. Add black beans and soaking water. Simmer 2 to 3 hours or until beans are soft.

Put soup in blender and puree until smooth. Return to pot, add other ingredients, and simmer for 15 minutes. If soup is too thin, thicken with 1 tablespoon arrowroot dissolved in a little water and simmer for a few more minutes until it thickens.

Bean Loaf

2 cups cooked beans, mashed
¼ cup bread crumbs or wheat germ (or combine)
2 Tbs. tomato sauce
¼ cup chopped onion
1 tsp. sea salt
1 tsp. Italian seasoning
1 tsp. kelp
Wheat germ for sprinkling
Preheat oven to 350°.

Combine all but last ingredient and pack into an oiled loaf pan. Sprinkle wheat germ on top and bake for 45 minutes, basting occasionally with oil.

Variation

Add chopped sautéed vegetables: mushrooms, string beans, carrots, etc.

Chapter 5

From Hamburgers to Soyburgers

When Oliver was four years old we took him to New York City to visit the top of the RCA Building. For lunch we promised to take him to the Alive Kitchen, an excellent vegetarian restaurant that has since closed.

On the way to the Alive Kitchen, we passed by the open back door of a well-known hamburger restaurant. The door led to the kitchen and the fumes hit us hard as we passed by on the street. "That's not an alive kitchen," Oliver said, "that's a dead kitchen!"

If people gave a little thought to what they are actually putting into their bodies when they eat a hamburger, smothered with ketchup and onions, often with a slice of yellow processed cheese, served in a bun made out of white processed flour, accompanied by chemically bleached potatoes fried in hydrogenated oil, sprinkled with commercial salt, and washed down with a cola mixture of sugar, caffeine, sodium benzoate, and coal tar derivatives, they might well come to their senses.

We have a vision of the not-too-distant-future when there is a health-food chain as big as the present fast-food chains. We look forward to the day when we can pull off the highway and go into a diner which serves sandwiches on whole grain breads instead of doughy white buns; salads with fresh vegetables and sprouts instead of pale lettuce with cottage cheese, Jell-o, and canned fruit (what they call a "health salad" in many roadside restaurants); fresh juices and spring water instead of colas and orangeade; nutritious beanburgers instead of hamburgers; and tamari sauce instead of ketchup.

The hot dog and hamburger will be remembered as symbols of America's pop culture. But for anyone who has made a commitment to health and nutrition, they would best be forgotten as food. Since Oliver and Jonathan were never "broken in" as babies to eat meat, there is no way we can get them to eat a hamburger or a hot dog, and we are well-pleased about that. You never know what kind of meat or meat by-products go into hamburgers. And hot dogs contain sodium nitrates and nitrites, which have been shown to be carcinogenic under certain circumstances. As Oliver has said many times, "That's no hot dog, that's a dead dog!"

So, until the Burger King becomes Beanburger King and we see Wimpy eating beanburgers instead of hamburgers, join us and make your own delicious beanburgers. They are easy to make and, if you like, you can prepare a large quantity and freeze them, placing sheets of waxed paper between them after they are shaped, and then wrapping them up in freezer wrap.

All of our beanburgers are high in protein, combining whole grains with beans. We serve them as a main course with a salad or steamed, nonstarchy vegetables. Beanburgers are also an excellent way to make use of any leftover grains and beans.

As always, our recipes are basic, so try them once our way and then feel free to experiment. There are so many interesting beanburger variations that recipes for these alone could fill up a book.

Basic Burger Recipe

We used to follow burger recipes until we discovered that there is a simple formula for making burgers from whatever we have on hand. We have burgers about twice a week and probably have not had the same burger twice in the last year, as there are so many possibilities for variation. Once you get the feeling for it, you won't even have to refer to this guide.

Foundation (one or more): cooked soybeans, navy beans, garbanzos, black beans, kidney beans, etc. Cooked brown rice, millet, kasha, cous-cous, bulghur

Vegetable Additions (one or more): Onions, celery, carrots, mushrooms, sprouts, etc.

Moistener and Binder: Eggs

Thickener (one or more): Bread crumbs, whole wheat flour, wheat bran, wheat germ, dry oatmeal, protein powder, ground nuts, cornmeal

Seasoning (one or more): Salt, pepper, parsley, garlic, thyme, sage, oregano, dill, tamari, miso

Grind, mash, or grate the basic foundation. Grate or sauté vegetables and add. Moisten mixture with egg. Thicken with one or more thickening ingredients. Add seasoning.

Shape into patties and dust with flour. Fry in oil over moderate heat until well browned on both sides.

Serve with Tahini Sauce (see Chapter 9), Whole Wheat Sauce (see Chapter 9), tamari, or tomato sauce.

Soyburgers

2 cups cooked soybeans
1 cup cooked brown rice
1 onion
1 carrot
1 stalk celery
2 cloves garlic
1½ tsp. thyme or dill weed
2 eggs
½ cup wheat germ

Mash soybeans and combine with brown rice. Finely chop onion, carrot, celery, and garlic. Add to soybean and rice mixture along with remaining ingredients and mix well. If mixture is not stiff enough, add more wheat germ.

Shape into patties and fry on both sides until well browned. Serve with Whole Wheat Sauce (see Chapter 9) or tamari.

Fritini Burgers

Fritini is a packaged, ready-made vegetarian burger product, imported from Switzerland. It is available at many supermarkets as well as health food stores. All you do is add water and you are ready to fry up a delicious burger. We use it as a base and add our own ingredients such as leftover grains or beans, mushrooms, onions, spices. You may also use a raw egg or chopped hard-boiled egg, and roll the burgers in wheat germ before frying.

Lentil Millet Patties

1 cup dried lentils
¾ cup whole hulled millet
1 onion chopped
salt and pepper to taste
2 eggs, lightly beaten
wheat germ
oil
tomato sauce

Put lentils in saucepan with water to cover. Bring to a boil and cook until tender, about 30 minutes.

Put millet and 1½ cups water in second saucepan, bring to a boil, cover, and simmer 30 minutes or until all water is absorbed.

Drain lentils and mix with millet. Add onion, salt, and pepper. Form into patties. Dip into beaten eggs and then into wheat germ.

Heat ¼ inch oil in heavy skillet and fry patties until golden. Drain on paper towels. Serve with tomato sauce.

Chapter 6

Macrobiotics: East Meets West

The term "macrobiotic" is derived from the Greek; *macro* means great, *bio* means vitality, and "biotics," the art of rejuvenation.

Macrobiotic cooking is derived from the traditional food preparation methods of ancient Japan, now preserved in Zen Buddhist monasteries. Zen monks are among the longest-lived and healthiest people in Japan.

The macrobiotic diet consists primarily of vegetarian foods, but also includes fish as a secondary food. The primary food at the meal is brown rice or another whole grain. Steamed or tempura fried vegetables make up the other part of the course. Tofu or bean curd is used frequently, as are other soybean dishes along with aduki and other beans.

Miso and tamari (which we shall discuss later in this chapter) are used for flavoring and added nutrition.

The purpose of the macrobiotic diet is to establish balance. According to Georges Osahwa, the founder of modern Zen Macrobiotics, everything that exists in the universe can be placed in one of two categories: Yin or Yang. Health and happiness can result from balancing these two forces. Yin is the expansive force and Yang is the contracting force. The ideal balance according to this diet is five parts Yin to one part Yang.

Yin and Yang can also be seen in chemical terms as acidity and alkalinity. Acid foods are rich in potassium and alkaline foods are rich in sodium.

These are the principles of macrobiotics, and if you wish to go further into the subject, as we hope you do, you'll find a listing of excellent reading in our bibliography. Most noteworthy of these books is *The Book of Macrobiotics* by Michio Kushi. But even if you do not wish to go deeper into macrobiotics, we think macrobiotic foods should be included in everybody's diet: they establish a nutritional balance that is hard to match.

In addition to its nutritional value, macrobiotic food can be an exquisite culinary experience. If you live in or near Boston, New York, Los Angeles, or San Francisco, you can easily find a macrobiotic restaurant and give it a try. Pick up a copy of *The East West Journal* and you'll find listings or advertisements for macrobiotic restaurants—in addition to a lot of interesting articles on macrobiotics and nutrition.

Macrobiotic cooking is extremely easy and rewarding in its basic form, as we are presenting it here. But it is also a very subtle art requiring skill and artistry to bring it to its culinary heights.

BASIC MACROBIOTIC COOKING

Brown Rice
Brown rice is the most perfectly balanced grain in the macrobiotic diet and one of the primary foods. See Chapter 3 for more about brown rice and how to prepare it.

Shoyu and Tamari
These are naturally fermented soy sauces which are aged in wood for one to two years. They are a delicious seasoning for soups, vegetables, whole grains, salads, and casseroles.

The commercial soy sauce products sold in supermarkets and usually served in Chinese restaurants differ in that they are not brewed or fermented but prepared from hydrolyzed vegetable protein by the reaction of defatted soybeans with hydrochloric acid. The flavor and coloring comes from additives such as corn syrup and caramel. Some varieties may contain sodium benzoate or alcohol preservatives.

Miso

Like yogurt, miso is a fermented food containing lactobacillus and other healthful microorganisms along with digestion-aiding enzymes. It has been used in Asia for over 2,500 years and is considered one of their most important soybean products. It is made from fermented soybeans and sea salt, or with an added grain like rice or barley.

Miso comes in many varieties, depending on its process of fermentation. Its range of flavors and colors, textures and aromas, is as varied as that of the world's fine cheeses and wines. You'll find at least one of the main varieties in most health food stores. Other stores like the Erewhon Store and Bread and Circus in Boston have several barrels of delicious varieties of miso. We feel that in the near future miso will be considered an essential element in America's cuisine and a basic seasoning to be found in kitchens across the country.

This all-purpose, high-protein seasoning can be used in many of the same ways we use salt. It can also be used as bouillon in soups and stews; in place of Worcestershire, ketchup, chutney, or relish; and in sauces, dips, and dressings.

Children may not take to its salty taste right away, especially if they are used to sweets, but it is worthwhile persisting in getting them to eat it because they will also come to love it. It's well that they do, for miso is an exceptional protein booster. An addition of a little miso to foods such as wheat, corn, and rice can result in large increases in usable protein.

Miso Soup

This is a delicious and healthy way to start a meal: the fermentation process of miso and its enzymes aids the digestion of the meal. There are an infinite variety of miso soup recipes. Here's one of our standards. We often take it along in a thermos on picnics and have it with whole-grain sandwiches.

2 sheets dry wakeme (sea vegetable available in some health food stores; optional)
1 onion, sliced
1 Tbs. sesame oil
4 cups water
2 scallions, sliced
4 Tbs. miso
Scallion for garnish

Rinse wakeme and soak for 15 minutes.

Sauté onion in oil in large saucepan or pot for 5 minutes. Add water and bring to a boil. Simmer for about 10 minutes. Cut the wakeme in small pieces and add to pot along with sliced scallions. Let simmer for another 10 minutes, then turn off the heat.

Dilute miso in a small amount of the soup and add to pot. Stir and cover pot and allow to steep for about 5 minutes. Garnish with tiny slices of raw scallions.

Variation

Use cabbage and other vegetables such as carrots and string beans. Sauté with onion and cook in soup for the full 20 minutes.

Miso Spread

Try this on top of a slice of good whole-grain bread.

1 Tbs. miso
4 Tbs. tahini
1 or 2 Tbs. water
1 tsp. grated orange peel

Mix miso, tahini, and water. Cook 5 minutes while stirring. When mixture thickens, mix in minced orange peel.

Nerimiso (Sweet Simmered Miso)

Nerimiso can be used as a sauce for grains, tofu, or vegetables, or served on the side of the plate and used as a chutney. It can also be used as a spread and is especially good on whole-grain unyeasted breads. To the recipe below you can add tahini, almond butter, or peanut butter, as well as such flavorings as ginger, grated lemon rind or orange rind, and so on.

5 Tbs. red or barley miso
$1\frac{1}{2}$ to $2\frac{1}{2}$ Tbs. honey
1 Tbs. water or $1\frac{1}{2}$ tsp. each of water and white wine

Combine all ingredients in a small skillet and heat. Simmer without boiling for 2 to 3 minutes over low heat, stirring constantly with a wooden spoon until mixture begins to thicken. Remove from heat and serve at room temperature. Refrigerate unused portion in a covered jar.

Chapter 7

Tofu: The Food of the Future – Discovered over Two Thousand Years Ago

Two thousand years ago in China one of the world's most nutritious, mineral-rich and protein-rich, easy-to-digest, and versatile foods was discovered: Its name is tofu. Tofu is as much a part of Oriental cookery as bread is in the West. What is tofu? Otherwise known as bean curd, tofu is an easily digestible "cheese" made from a coagulation of soy milk.

In Japan today there are some 38,000 tofu shops, and it is estimated that more than 900 million people in East Asia include tofu as an indispensable food in their diet. It is used in much the same way that meat and dairy products are used in the dietary pattern of the West.

The protein efficiency of soybeans is the primary reason why tofu has played such a key role in the daily diet of the people of East Asia. According to the tables of NPU (Net Protein Utilization) given in the book *Diet for a Small Planet*, the protein in tofu is equal in our bodies to the protein in chicken.

Not only is tofu a valuable source of complete high-quality protein, it is also a remarkable protein booster. It contains an abundance of lysine, an essential amino acid that is lacking in many grain products. Most grains, on the other hand, are endowed with amino acids that are present but limited in soybeans; thus they complement each other perfectly. By serving tofu together with whole-grain bread or brown rice, the protein boost can be considerable. If you serve 3½ ounces of tofu together with 1¼ cups of brown rice, 32 percent more protein is obtained than if you serve them separately.

Tofu is easy to digest. It is prepared by a process that carefully removes the crude fiber and water-soluble carbohydrates from soybeans. Thus, it is an excellent food for babies, elderly adults, and people with digestive problems.

Tofu is also the ideal diet food. An 8-ounce serving contains only 147 calories (about ¼ as many as beef, and ⅓ the calories of eggs). It has one of the lowest ratios of calories to protein found in any known plant food.

Tofu, in addition to being low in calories, is low in saturated fats and is free of cholesterol. It contains high amounts of lecithin and linoleic acids, which help to eliminate deposits of cholesterol from the vital organs and bloodstream.

Tofu is also an excellent source of calcium. When solidified with calcium chloride nigari or calcium sulfate, tofu contains 23 percent more calcium by weight than milk. And kinugoshi, which is similar to tofu and is discussed in the recipe section, contains 50 percent more calcium by weight than milk.

Tofu is a good source of other minerals such as iron, phosphorus, potassium, and sodium, of essential B vitamins, and of choline and fat-soluble vitamin E.

Considering what an incredibly healthful, versatile, and efficient food tofu is, it's a wonder that most Americans (perhaps even yourself) have never even heard about it. What is even more astonishing is that America now produces about two-thirds of the world's supply of soybeans. If all the soybeans harvested in the United States in a year were used to make tofu, they would provide each American with enough protein for three years. But where does all this protein now go? About 95 percent of all un-exported soy protein ends up as feed for livestock, and of this, 77 to 95 percent is lost in the process of animal metabolism. The price of meat is getting higher and higher and in the coming decades it could reach a point where only the very rich will be able to afford it.

Most experts now consider soybeans to be the most promising source of low-cost, high-quality protein available in large enough quantities to meet human needs on a worldwide scale.

Although preparing tofu can seem a bit complicated at first and it does take time to prepare (a steady hour), we are certain that the rewards of making your own tofu will more than compensate for your time and effort.

Once you make your own tofu or buy it in a health food or oriental food store, the varieties of serving it are countless. For many delicious gourmet recipes, refer to *The Book of Tofu* by William Shurtleff and Akiko Aoyagi, published by Autumn Press. *The Book of Tofu* has 500 recipes ranging from deep-fried tofu with barbecue sauce to strawberry tofu pie. The book is fascinating reading (much of our information about tofu was adapted from it) and is worth buying for the beautiful illustrations alone.

Before getting on to the making of tofu, we would like to leave you with a quote from *The Book of Tofu*: "The Chinese say that sages, yogis, and monks, who rely for sustenance on nothing but the mists of heaven and the fresh morning dew, are particularly fond of tofu as their third choice."

Quick Tofu

4 cups water
1 cup full fat soy flour
4 Tbs. lemon juice

Bring water to boil in large pot. In the meantime mix the soy flour with enough cold water to make a paste. Beat for at least a minute with egg beater. Add to boiling water, stirring constantly. Reduce heat and simmer for 5 minutes. Add lemon juice, then set aside to cool.

Strain the curds through a fine sieve or cheesecloth. This is similar in taste to traditional tofu, but the texture is softer, more like cottage cheese.

Try adding some chopped-up garlic, parsley, and chives to the tofu, seasoning with vegetable salt.

Homemade Traditional Tofu

Making tofu the traditional way may seem very complicated at first, but we do hope you attempt it. We cannot overemphasize the nutritional value of tofu as well as its culinary potential. It will take an hour of steady cooking, and you will find it helpful, although not necessary, to have a partner.

In the list of utensils you will need, below, is a "settling box." This container, which can also be described as a flat-bottomed, rectangular colander, can be made by drilling holes the size of a pencil in a loaf pan. It can also be made out of wood, or you can buy a very nicely crafted one, made from kiln-dried Philippine mahogany. It is included in a "Tofu Kit" and is sold in some health food stores or may be ordered from The Learning Tree, Box 829, Corte Madera, California 94925. The kit also includes a pressing sack, cheesecloth, natural nigari solidifier, and a handy 16-page instruction and recipe book, from which we borrowed the following recipe for preparing homemade tofu.

Start with a clean kitchen, assemble all utensils and ingredients, and read through the entire process at least once before beginning to work.

Utensils

coarsely woven cotton dishcloth ("pressing sack")
large, round-bottomed colander (that will fit into pressing pot)
measuring cup
"pressing pot" (6 to 8 quarts), or basin
large cooking pot with lid (10 to 12 quarts)
electric blender or food processer
long-handled wooden spoon
potato masher or sturdy 1-quart jar for pressing
2-quart saucepan or bowl
measuring spoons
2-foot square cheesecloth
settling box with lid
fine-mesh strainer
shallow ladle or dipper, or a large spoon

Ingredients

16 cups water
1½ cups soybeans, soaked in 2 quarts water for 10 to 12 hours
solidifier: any one of the following may be used:
    1½ to 1¼ tsp. natural nigari
    2½ tsp. Epsom salts
    5 Tbs. lemon juice
    4 Tbs. apple cider vinegar

1. Moisten pressing sack and line colander with it. Set lined colander in mouth of pressing pot.
2. Put 6½ cups of water (hot if possible) in cooking pot and place it, uncovered, on stove over high heat.
3. While water is heating, divide drained beans into two equal portions. Combine one portion with 2½ cups cold water in blender. Cover and blend at high speed for 3 minutes or until very smooth consistency. Empty mixture into water heating in cooking pot and repeat the procedure with remaining beans and 2½ more cups water. Use approximately ¼ cup of cold water to retrieve what bean mixture remains in blender and also add that to cooking pot. With wooden spatula or spoon, stir sides and bottom of cooking pot frequently to prevent sticking. If using a food mill, grind beans without addition of cold water and instead add 4 more cups of water to cooking pot.
4. When foam suddenly rises in cooking pot, turn off heat, remove pot from stove, and pour contents into pressing sack, where it will go through the colander into pressing pot. Quickly scrub out cooking pot with *cold* water and return it to stove.
5. With one hand, twist mouth of pressing sack closed and with the other hand, press sack against colander, with a sturdy jar or potato masher to extract as much soy milk as possible. *Caution:* Don't burn yourself! Shake solids in pressing sack to bottom and press again.
6. Open mouth of pressing sack and sprinkle 3 cups of cold water over the solids, stir, twist the sack closed and again press as much soy milk out of the pressing sack as possible with jar or your hands to squeeze the last liquid from pressing sack.
7. Remove pressing sack and colander, then pour the liquid in pressing pot back into clean, empty cooking pot on stove. Heat over high heat, stirring frequently, until liquid

begins to boil. (This usually takes a while, so be patient.) Reduce heat to medium-high and simmer for 7 minutes. This is a good time to clean up behind yourself, using *cold* water. Empty solids from pressing sack and reserve for making granola, thickening soups, baking, or feeding to animals. Wash sack, wring it out and hang it to dry.

8. Measure nigari or other curdling agent into measuring cup and dissolve completely with 1 cup of cold water.

9. Turn off heat under soy milk and remove pot from burner. With a wooden spoon, immediately stir soy milk vigorously a few times and, while stirring, pour in ⅓ cup of solidifier solution (nigari and water). Continue stirring a few more times, being careful to reach bottom and sides of pot. (Tofu curdles from the bottom up.) Now, stop wooden spoon in soy milk and wait until liquid movement ceases. Remove spoon and pour another ⅓ cup of solidifier solution over back of the spoon, using it to disperse solution so that it falls like rain over surface of the soy milk. Cover pot and wait 3 minutes. (Here's more cleanup time.)

10. Stir remaining solidifier solution, remove pot lid, and using the back of wooden spoon, disperse last ⅓ cup of solidifier solution over surface of soy milk, then gently and slowly stir top ½ inch of soy milk for about 15 seconds, cover pot, and wait 3 more minutes (6 minutes if using Epsom salts). Uncover and stir soy milk surface again for 20 to 30 seconds or until all milky liquid is curdled. (White curds should now be floating in yellowish whey.) If any milky uncurdled liquid remains, wait 1 minute, then stir gently 1 inch deep until curdled. If milky liquid persists, dissolve one-quarter of the original amount of nigari (or other solidifier) in ⅓ cup of water and pour directly onto uncurdled portions; stir gently until curdled.

11. Dampen cheesecloth and use it to line inside of the settling box, draping excess over sides. Set box over a pan or on a sink drainboard.

12. Place cooking pot in sink next to settling box and gently press fine strainer into pot so that several cups of whey fill strainer and curds are held out. Using shallow ladle, ladle hot whey out of strainer. Pour whey over cheesecloth, saturating cloth thoroughly so that it clings tightly to inside surfaces of settling box. Use up as much whey as possible. Remove strainer.

13. Now gently ladle curds and remaining whey into box in layers. Fold edges of cloth neatly over curds. Place box lid, handles up, on box; set a light weight (a jar of water is fine) on lid and allow curds to press for 10 to 15 minutes. The longer the pressing, the firmer the tofu.

14. Fill sink with cold water. Remove weight and submerge pressing box in cold water. Remove top of box and invert it. Push wrapped tofu out of box and into sink.

15. Remove box from sink. Unwrap tofu by letting its weight pull it away from cheesecloth as you slowly lift cheesecloth out of sink. (Be careful not to pull cheesecloth too sharply or it will pull away with some tofu attached.) The tofu cake will settle slowly to the bottom of the water.

16. With a sharp knife, underwater, cut tofu in half crosswise. Using a plate for support, slide each half of tofu out of water and set plate at an angle for tofu to drain.

17. Rinse cheesecloth and wring it out. Scrub sections of box and strainer and set pressing sack and cheesecloth in sun (if possible) to dry and freshen. The box can also be sun freshened, *but not until it has thoroughly dried in the shade.*

Your tofu is now ready to eat!

Tofu Sandwich

Our son Oliver recently invented a tofu sandwich. He cut a cold piece of tofu, placed it between two slices of whole wheat bread, added some mayonnaise and lettuce, seasoned it with Spike, and unknowingly created a high-protein sandwich. Oliver's Tofu Sandwich is now regularly served in our house. Tofu served in this manner tastes remarkably like a cheese sandwich.

Cold or fried, tofu can also be served in pita bread pockets, with salad, sprouts, and tahini, mayonnaise, or other sauces.

Tofu Salad

Cut cold, bite-sized pieces of tofu and add it to your favorite salad. Try it with lettuce, alfalfa sprouts, and cherry tomatoes with a tahini-lemon dressing or French dressing.

Tofu and Peas

For a very quick meal, mix slices of tofu with frozen peas and sauté them in a wok. Serve over or alongside brown rice, millet, or kasha. You can also add the cooked grain to the wok after the peas are cooked and heat it all up together. Season with tamari. Curry, garlic, onion, and other spices can also be added to this simple dish.

Tofu and Snow Peas

This is a beautiful looking as well as delicious tasting combination. Sauté Chinese snow peas in a wok with a little garlic and ginger added to the oil. Add the tofu and continue to sauté. Season with a little salt and/or tamari. Serve with millet or cous-cous.

Tofu and Chinese Vegetables

Follow instructions for wok cooking vegetables in Chapter 2 and add tofu as a last ingredient.

Tofu and Bean Sprouts

Wok fry tofu and mung bean sprouts in oil with a little garlic. Season with tamari in wok.

Tofu and Sesame

Sauté tofu in 1 to 2 tablespoons of sesame oil. Sprinkle sesame seeds onto tofu in wok. Serve on brown rice. Add a little tahini (sesame butter) to the oil and seeds that remain on the bottom of wok and spoon over tofu and rice.

KINUGOSHI

Kinugoshi is very similar to tofu, except that the whey is not removed; therefore it has more of the nutrients originally in the soybean. Although it is not as versatile in cooking as tofu, it is easier and faster to prepare and requires no special settling box. *Kinu* means silk in Japan, where kinugoshi's cool silk taste is considered a delicacy.

There are five different types of kinugoshi sold in Japan, all prepared different ways with different solidifiers. In addition to the different types, there are many different methods of serving it. Presented here is Custard Style Kinugoshi, adapted from *The Book of Tofu*.

Custard Style Kinugoshi

3½ cups Soy Milk (see Chapter 4)
solidifier: ½ tsp. granulated nigari, or
        ½ tsp. Epsom salts, or
        4 tsp. lemon juice, or
        1 Tbs. apple cider vinegar
2 Tbs. water

Place bowl on a firm surface and pour in freshly made, hot soy milk. In a small cup, quickly mix solidifier with 2 tablespoons water and stir until dissolved. Stir soy milk back and forth briskly for 3 to 5 seconds, then quickly pour in all of the solidifier solution. Continue stirring soy milk for 3 to 5 seconds more, making sure to stir the bottom of the bowl.

Now stop spoon upright in center of soy bean milk and wait until turbulence ceases. Lift out spoon. Let mixture stand for 20 to 30 minutes while it cools and solidifies. Cover and refrigerate.

Serve as is, using it as a high-protein pickup during the day or enjoying it as a side dish with brown rice. Or sweeten with a little honey or flavor with tamari or miso. A spoonful of tahini may be added for taste and nutrition.

TEMPEH

In addition to tofu, another high-protein soybean food that may have an important role in nutritious diets in the near future is tempeh. Tempeh has been a staple protein in Southeast Asia for centuries. Whereas tofu is made by curdling, tempeh is made by natural fermentation.

Fermented foods, such as yogurt, sauerkraut, soy sauce, miso, and sourdough bread, are very healthful and should be included in everybody's diet. Fermentation produces lactic acid, which destroys harmful intestinal bacteria and contributes toward the digestion and assimilation of vitamins and other nutrients.

We were introduced to tempeh at a health food convention, where it was displayed at the Farm Foods booth. Farm Foods are produced on The Farm, a 1,750-acre vegetarian community in Summertown, Tennessee. The tempeh was sautéed and to us had the taste and texture of veal cutlets. Others remarked that it tasted like sausages, fried chicken, shrimp, and fried egg. We brought a Farm Foods Tempeh Kit home, prepared basic tempeh, then fried up delicious tempeh burgers and tempeh cutlet parmesan.

Making tempeh is easy, much like making yogurt. The ingredients are split and hulled soybeans, tempeh starter, and vinegar. To prepare tempeh, you will need an incubator where the soybeans can ferment. A stable temperature close to 90 degrees is required. An oven with a pilot light can work well, if the temperature is above 90 degrees. Otherwise a simple incubator can be constructed from plans included in the Farm Foods Tempeh Kit.

The Tempeh Kit, including starter and instructions, and split, hulled soybeans is now available in health foods stores or by mail order from: Farm Foods, P. O. Box 156, Summertown, Tenn. 38483.

The June 1977 issue of *Prevention Magazine* featured an article about tempeh, if you are interested in reading further.

Chapter 8

"Open Sesame": The Magic of Seeds and Nuts

In the story "Ali Baba and the Forty Thieves," Ali Baba discovers the magic words "Open sesame" that open the entrance to a treasure of riches beyond measure. No less magical are the powers that lie within the seed itself. Seeds are the patterns of life for trees, plants, and vegetation. The life principle and all the necessary elements to start even such a massive tree as the redwood are contained in a seed.

Seeds found in Tutankhamen's tomb, over three thousand years old, are reported to have grown when put in soil. Flower seeds from missions hundreds of years old have grown when planted.

Seeds contain nearly every single food element that has been discovered. They are the highest source of protein in the vegetable kingdom. Because seeds have so much nutritional value, we try to use them in one form or another in our daily diet.

We eat them whole as a snack or sprinkled on salads. We grind them in a nut mill and sprinkle the powder on cereal or add it to beanburgers, breads, and protein loaves. We mix them with honey and fruits and make candies and desserts. The main seeds we use are sesame, sunflower, and pumpkin, and we will occasionally use flax and chia seeds as well.

Seeds have a high oil content and can become rancid, so it is important to buy them fresh and keep them refrigerated, if possible. It is also best to grind them just prior to use, as the outer hull protects the nutritional value and guards against rancidity.

Light and oxygen have a depleting effect on the vitamin content of seeds. If you don't keep seeds in the refrigerator, try to keep them in a cool, dark place. Dark brown bottles help to protect them from exposure to light.

SESAME SEEDS

Sesame seeds contain almost 50 percent more protein than meat and nearly twice as much calcium as milk. They are rich in phosphorus, niacin, and vitamin E. These seeds are rich in lecithin and fatty acids that help dissolve cholesterol. It's been said that heart disease and incidence of heart attacks are low in the Mid-Eastern countries that include sesame seeds in their daily diet.

Sesame seeds can be purchased raw, hulled, or toasted. The raw are more nutritious and the toasted taste better. We use them both. We add whole sesame seeds to cereals, cookies, vegetable casseroles, and on bread crusts. These small seeds must be properly chewed when eaten whole or they will pass right through your body unassimilated.

Sesame can be made into a wonderful milk-substitute drink that is easily digested.

Our favorite use for sesame is tahini, which is a sesame seed butter with a more flowing consistency than peanut butter. It has been said that 2 tablespoons of tahini is equivalent in protein to a 16-ounce steak. It is digested and assimilated into the bloodstream in less than a quarter of an hour, whereas it takes 2 to 5 hours to digest, assimilate, and metabolize meat.

You can make your own tahini, but we prefer to buy ours. Our favorite brands here on the East coast are Infinity and Erewhon. Their consistency is smooth and creamy. Westbrae on the West coast also makes a good tahini. Some tahinis are much thicker and require a lot of stirring and the addition of oil to bring them to a flowing consistency.

Tahini mixed with honey, maple syrup, or apple butter makes a delicious spread for breads. It also makes a good topping for fruit salads, ice cream, and other desserts. Mixed with tamari, it is delicious over vegetables and grains, particularly brown rice. Mixed with lemon juice, it makes a delicious salad dressing and sauce for felafels. A word of caution: tahini is a highly concentrated food, so be careful not to eat too much of it. I got so hooked on it when I first ate it that I finished half a jar the first day.

Quick Tahini Sauce

Mix a little of each: tahini, water, tamari. Stir until smooth.

Tahini Yogurt

To each serving of yogurt, add 1 to 3 tablespoons tahini. Sweeten with honey, maple syrup, apple butter, apple concentrate, or fructose. For a thicker, crunchier treat, add wheat germ, coconut, and chopped pecans.

Tahini Salad Dressing I

1 cup tahini
½ cup lemon juice
1 Tbs. honey (optional)
Blend all ingredients until smooth. Use less lemon juice if you like it less tangy and add water if you like it thinner.

Tahini Salad Dressing II

½ cup tahini
¼ cup oil
½ tsp. sea salt
juice of ½ lemon
½ cup water
2 pinches thyme or tarragon
1 tsp. tamari
Mix tahini, oil, salt, and lemon juice. Add water gradually, stirring smooth as you add it. Add herbs and tamari and mix well.

Tahini Bread Spread

Tahini and honey or tahini and apple butter make a delicious, rich spread. Try it on whole wheat or seven-grain toast.

Tahini Ice Cream Sundae

Pour 1 tablespoon of tahini over a scoop of vanilla ice cream. Sprinkle over that a teaspoon of wheat germ, some shredded coconut (optional), and chopped almonds. Top with a little honey or Hot Blueberry Sauce (see Chapter 11).

Sesame Salt (Gomasio)

We consider gomasio one of the more important recipes in the book, as it adds the nutrition of sesame seeds while providing an unusually salty taste for the limited amount of salt it contains. It has become an essential seasoning on our table. Once you try it, you'll never want to be without it. It is delicious over vegetables or cooked grains.

10 Tbs. sesame seeds

1 Tbs. sea salt

Stir-roast seeds in dry pan over medium heat. Combine with salt in mortar or nut grinder and grind until powdery. Store in covered container and use in place of salt.

Kelp Salt

Here is another highly nutritious salt combination. Combine equal parts of granulated kelp and sea salt and use in place of salt.

SUNFLOWER SEEDS

In the sunflower, nature has produced an extraordinarily beautiful plant that has inspired such artists as Van Gogh, Gauguin, and Cezanne.

It is called a sunflower not only because it resembles a sunburst, but also because it has the amazing ability to follow and face the sun from morning to night. In addition to absorbing a maximum amount of solar energy, the sunflower also has an extensive root system that goes down deep into the ground to extract trace minerals not found in topsoil. Sunflower seeds are therefore endowed with ample amounts of phosphorus, calcium, iron, fluorine, iodine, potassium, magnesium, zinc, thiamine, niacin, vitamins D and E, unsaturated fatty acids, and protein.

We eat sunflower seeds as they are or mixed with nuts and raisins for a snack. We also sprinkle them over vegetable and fruit salads. Sunflower meal, ground in a nut grinder, adds nutritional value to baked goods, protein loaves, burgers, and seed milk.

PUMPKIN SEEDS

We use pumpkin seeds in the same way as sunflower seeds. They are rich in iron, protein, unsaturated fats, phosphorus, and calcium.

Toasted Sunflower and Pumpkin Seeds

Coat bottom of frying pan with oil; spread out pumpkin or sun-flower seeds, or combination of both, and stir-fry over medium flame until slightly browned. Or put seeds in oiled cookie pan and place in oven until browned. Salt to taste. Or add some tamari as you stir-fry for tamari-toasted seeds.

FLAXSEED

Flaxseed is a natural laxative. Leave a tablespoon of flaxseed in a glass of water to soak overnight and then drink it about a half-hour before breakfast. Or brew it into a tea by boiling it in a pint of water to one tablespoon of flaxseed. Boil for about 6 minutes and strain. For added cleansing benefit, add a little lemon juice.

You can also grind flaxseed into a meal and sprinkle it on your breakfast cereal.

CHIA SEED

There is an element of mystique surrounding the tiny, blackish chia seed. It was used in ancient India and by the Indians of Mexico and the United States as an energizer. It has been recognized for centuries as an energy and endurance food. For best assimilation, grind the seed just before use and sprinkle up to a tablespoon over salads, vegetables, cereals, and in soups, sauces, and drinks. Chia tastes mild and pleas-ant, like flaxseed meal.

SPROUTS

Sprouts are the freshest, most alive food we can put in our bodies. If we had to single out one food as the most important in this book, we would probably choose sprouts.

Wherever you live, you can become a gardener of delicious, unsprayed, organic sprouts. All you need is a wide-mouthed glass jar, the space for a small pan, cheesecloth or nylon or wire mesh, water, and a warm corner, and you can watch life unfold before you.

When seeds sprout, their chemistry changes. Their nutritional value is improved; they acquire chlorophyl and vitamins A and C. Sprouts also maintain the high protein content of the seed while the starch content is reduced.

How to Sprout

Here's what you'll need:

A wide-mouthed quart glass bottle (preferably a mason jar with a removable inner metal top.

Three grades of nylon mesh (available in fabric stores), extra fine, fine, and medium; or wire mesh; or cheesecloth.

You can also buy a ready-made sprouting kit at your health food store.

And this is all you do:

Place the seeds in jar and fill with water to soak overnight. Use 2 tablespoons of alfalfa seed, 6 of mung beans.

The following morning place the fine mesh over the top of the jar, securing it in place with the open mason top or a rubber band. Drain off the soak water and fill with fresh water, then drain again. Place the jar on its side, spreading seeds out, and keep in a warm, dark corner.

Rinse every morning and evening. As the sprouts grow and throw off the seed hulls, change to a larger-screen top so you can rinse hulls away. With alfalfa seeds you can probably stay with a fine screen, but for the mung beans you will need a coarser screen to let the hulls get through.

Sprouts develop in 3 to 5 days. When the first young leaves appear, place in direct sunlight for the development of chlorophyl. Wait about 8 hours after the last rinsing before refrigerating in a closed container.

The alfalfa seed is one of the easiest and best seeds to sprout. It is one of the most complete and nutritionally rich foods. In addition to its high potency of vitamins and minerals, it is high in protein and contains every essential amino acid. And alfalfa sprouts are delicious. We use them in salads and on sandwiches in place of lettuce.

Lentil and mung bean sprouts are also among our favorites. Sprouted mixtures of alfalfa, mung beans, and lentils are available in some health food stores, or you can make your own. They make an excellent combination. Mung bean sprouts are the ones that you get in Chinese restaurants. They are a bit tough to eat raw, and we prefer to steam them or stir-fry them in the wok.

Among the other seeds and beans that can be sprouted are soybeans, barley, buckwheat, fava, lima, pinto, corn, cress, clover, caraway, celery, dill, flax, fenugreek, garbanzos, kale, lettuce, millet, parsley, pumpkin, oats, sunflower, safflower, and wheat.

Wheat grass sprouts have been getting a lot of recognition for healing properties attributed to their high chlorophyl content. The Hippocrates Health Center in Boston has treated cancer and other diseases with wheat grass therapy. For more information on wheat grass and other sprouts, pick up the book, *Survival Into the 21st Century* by Viktoras Kulvinskas, or write the Hippocrates Health Center, 25 Exeter Street, Boston, Massachusetts 02116.

Sprout Salad

2 cups bean sprouts
2 cups alfalfa sprouts
1 cup raw mushrooms, sliced vertically
½ cup chopped walnuts
Combine ingredients and serve with Avocado Dressing (see below).

Avocado Dressing

2 avocados, peeled and mashed
1 tomato, skinned and sliced
½ cup lemon juice
1 Tbs. honey (optional)
spices and seasonings to your own taste
Blend ingredients until smooth.

Sprout Salad in Yogurt

1 cup mung bean sprouts
1 cup alfalfa sprouts
1 cup diced cucumber
½ cup chopped walnuts
4 cups yogurt

Mix all ingredients. Season to taste with sea salt and kelp. Or sweeten with honey.

ALMONDS

Almonds are the "King of Nuts." They are an excellent source of high-quality protein and are high in calcium, phosphorus, iron, and niacin, thus are an exceptional food for building teeth and bones. Almonds also contain a good amount of B vitamins.

Ground almonds can be sprinkled over cereals, soups, and salads. After grinding nuts, be sure to keep them in an airtight glass container and in a cool, dark place, preferably the refrigerator. Almonds can also be made into nut butter and into a nut milk for children.

It's best to purchase almonds raw. If you like them roasted, you can easily do it yourself by coating the nuts with a tiny amount of vegetable oil and placing them in the oven for a few minutes. When they are roasted, sprinkle on a little sea salt. You can also sprinkle on a small amount of tamari before roasting for delicious tamari-roasted almonds.

Almond Milk

1 cup almonds, blanched
1 quart water
1 to 2 Tbs. honey
pinch of salt
1 Tbs. oil

Blend all ingredients until smooth. Strain for finer milk. *Note:* To blanch almonds, pour boiling water over them and let stand for a couple of minutes. Then you can slip the skins off with your fingers.

Variations
Almond Cashew Milk: Use equal parts of almonds and cashews.
Almond Sesame Milk: Use equal parts of almonds and sesame seeds.

PEANUTS

Peanuts are not really nuts but, rather, legumes. By themselves, they are not a complete protein, but combined with grains and other seeds they make up a high-quality protein. This happens naturally if you make a peanut butter sandwich on whole wheat bread. Peanut butter is also delicious and protein-rich when it is served on rice cakes. Another way of completing the protein in peanut butter is to mix it with tahini.

If you like peanuts, eat them in moderation, since they are acid-forming.

Commercial peanut butters are made with hydrogenated oils, as well as with other additives. All it takes is a little stirring when the oil separates in natural peanut butter. If the peanut butter gets dry toward the bottom of the jar, add a little extra oil (safflower oil is preferred) and mix it in.

CASHEWS

Cashews also are not really nuts, but seeds of the cashew apple. They are a good source of vitamin D, iron, thiamine, protein, and fat. Purchase cashews raw and if you like them roasted, do it yourself.

Raw cashews are soft, so they can be blended to a smooth white liquid and used in many recipes. Because of their softness, we gave our children cashews as their first nut. Cashew milk is excellent for children and can be used in place of milk in many recipes.

Cashew Milk

1 cup raw cashews
1 quart water
1 Tbs. soy oil
2 Tbs. honey or maple syrup
¼ tsp. salt
Blend ingredients well until smooth. This can be used in recipes in place of whole milk.

Banana Cashew Milkshake

1 cup Cashew Milk (see preceding recipe)
1 ripe banana
1 tsp. honey
1 tsp. oil
1 tsp. vanilla
Blend all ingredients until smooth.
Try also using other fruits: blueberries, strawberries, etc.

Chapter 9

Sauce as a Source of Nutrition

In most cuisines, sauces are used primarily for adding flavor and appetite appeal to the dishes. In our cuisine, however, we prepare foods for our whole body as well as our taste buds. Our sauces add nutrition in addition to enhancing flavor.

Many of the sauces that are used in the traditional Western diets are not only nutritionally weak, but also poorly combined with the foods they are served with; these can result in ill health when used frequently.

Spaghetti with tomato sauce is one example of a combination that is not ideal. Tomatoes are acid fruits, and when eaten with refined starches such as spaghetti, macaroni, or bread, cause acidity and fermentation in the digestive system. N. W. Walker, in his book *Diet and Salad Suggestions*, cites that the tendency toward ulcerations in the intestinal tract among the Latin races has been attributed to the excessive use of tomatoes in combination with concentrated starch products, and he states that these ulcerated conditions have been relieved when these incompatible combinations were eliminated from the diet.

Also many sauces that are too frequently used in the American diet contain cheese and cream, saturated fats, eggs, and other ingredients that add up in calories, carbohydrates, and cholesterol.

Nutritional sauces provide a healthy alternative.

Whole Wheat Sauce

2 Tbs. butter or oil
2 Tbs. whole wheat flour
1 cup water or stock
2 Tbs. tamari
2 Tbs. Vegebase (available at health food stores)

Slowly heat butter in sauce pan until melted. Add flour and stir until well mixed. Add water or stock, a little at a time. Last, add tamari and Vegebase. Simmer for a few minutes.

Ginger Tamari Sauce

¼ cup tamari
¼ cup lemon juice
4 Tbs. honey
1 tsp. grated ginger

Combine all ingredients. Pour over vegetables or use as a dip for tempura vegetables.

Tahini Sauce

½ cup tahini
¼ cup water
¼ cup lemon juice
1 clove garlic
¼ tsp. sea salt

Blend ingredients thoroughly. This is especially good on felafel.

Onion Tahini Sauce

3 onions, chopped
1 clove garlic, minced
5 Tbs. tahini
2 Tbs. tamari
1 tsp. ground cumin

Sauté onions and garlic in oil. Add tahini, tamari, and cumin. Stir until smooth. Thin with water if desired. Goes great on kasha, brown rice, etc.

Chapter 10

Say "Cheese," But Not Too Often

Vegetarians who include dairy products in their diet are called "lacto-vegetarians." Milk and cheese products are mucus-forming and hard to eliminate from the body, so we think it is best to eat them in moderation. Whenever we feel a cold coming on, we eliminate dairy completely.

If you do eat dairy foods, we recommend that you include cleansing foods in your diet. We squeeze half a lemon in a glass of warm water and drink it in the morning upon arising. In addition to having cleansing properties, this drink is a tonic. We also use lemon juice in our salad dressings in place of vinegar.

There are many herbal teas that are valuable cleansers, one of the most popular being camomile. Raw vegetable juices such as carrot, beet, spinach, horseradish, celery, and cucumber are also very helpful.

We now have milk occasionally without overindulging in it. Most of the time we use skim or low-fat milk. When we drink whole milk we try to get raw certified milk. Although it is much more expensive, it is far superior in taste and nutrition. In addition, the cows on certified raw dairy farms are carefully inspected and well taken care of, whereas the cattle of commercial dairies are likely to be heavily injected with antibiotics. These drugs often pass through the milk and are not eliminated by the pasteurization process.

Goat's milk is said to be closer in composition to human milk than is cow's milk. There are also goat milk cheeses, yogurt, and honey-sweetened ice cream.

CHEESE

When we traveled through France we often enjoyed a slice of Camembert or Brie, but when we returned to the United States the cheese never tasted quite as delicious as it did in France. We chalked it up to the lack of that wonderful French countryside atmosphere until we discovered that the cheese we ate in France was unpasteurized. Like milk, cheese loses a good deal of nutritional value and flavor in pasteurization. In America, raw milk cheeses are available in health food stores. They are a bit expensive, but well worth the price. We like raw milk cheddar cheese or Monterey Jack served on a slice of rich whole wheat bread and topped with alfalfa sprouts.

In the supermarket, we generally select cheeses such as cottage, farmer, Norwegian Jarlsberg, Swiss, Swedish Farmer, Danish Gjetost, English Cheshire, New Zealand cheddar, and Vermont cheddar. There is a good chapter on cheeses in *The Supermarket Handbook* by Nikki and David Goldbeck. It is a highly informative book about how to find the most natural, healthful products in the supermarket, with specific brand recommendations.

BUTTERMILK

As a child, I had the same impression of buttermilk as comedian Shelley Berman when he said, "It's not the buttermilk I don't like, it's the way the glass looks when you're through drinking it!"

But when I got to Sweden, I tasted *filmjölk,* which is very similar to buttermilk, and I loved it. The Swedes, however, do not drink it out of a glass. They serve it in bowls, plain or on top of cereals with blueberries or strawberries. When I got back home, I became a buttermilk fan and poured it over my granola instead of milk. If you find it a bit sour, you can sweeten it with honey.

Unfortunately, it is hard to find the old-fashioned, churned kind. Most buttermilks today are made artificially in the dairy plants. If you do come across the old-fashioned, churned buttermilk, you are in for a real treat.

YOGURT

Of all the dairy foods, we rank yogurt as supreme. It is a predigested food that is valuable to people of all ages.

Yogurt is one of the oldest health foods. The ancient Hebrews ate yogurt, as did the Egyptians. In the Book of Genesis there is mention that Abraham ate yogurt and served it to his guests. Yogurt is a staple of the Bulgarians, who eat it daily and have one of the highest rates of longevity in the world.

Yogurt contains certain bacteria which work in the intestinal tract to break down milk sugar into lactic acid in which disease-producing bacteria are unable to live. Lacto bacillius, the beneficial bacteria in yogurt, manufactures generous amounts of B vitamins in the digestive tract where they are quickly absorbed and distributed throughout the body.

Yogurt is also beneficial to anyone with a sensitive stomach as it is much more digestible than milk.

Aside from all its health benefits, yogurt is a delicious food and an excellent ingredient in recipes. It is very easy to make your own yogurt without any fancy gadgets and you'll find our recipe below.

Be wary of yogurt manufacturers who advertise their yogurt as "all natural" when they contain fruit preserves that are made with large quantities of refined sugar. We do not consider white sugar a natural product by any means and it is best to buy yogurt plain and flavor it yourself. Plain, unflavored yogurt is truly delicious when you get used to its natural taste.

Oliver one day discovered that he could make his own Dutch apple yogurt by adding unsweetened apple sauce and cinnamon. Jonathan likes fresh or frozen blueberries in his yogurt. Let your child taste plain yogurt before you lay your sweet tooth on him. If you must sweeten, add a little honey or grate in fresh apples, pears, or other sweet fruits. When Oliver and Jonathan were babies, we put plain yogurt in the blender along with apples, pears, or bananas.

Following are some of our dairy recipes. But remember to eat dairy in moderation.

Safflower Butter

If you like butter but want to cut down on it, here is a spread you can make that combines the unsaturated fat of safflower oil. Or you may use sunflower oil.

1 pound butter, softened
1 cup safflower oil

Blend oil and butter and pour into a container. Chill. Makes about 3 cups.

Open-Faced Avocado Cheese Sandwich

1 slice seven-grain bread (or sprouted whole wheat bread)
¼ ripe avocado, mashed
1 slice cheese (Swiss, Jarlsberg, cheddar, or Monterey Jack)
Spike, to taste
1 tsp. sesame seeds

Toast bread lightly in toaster. Spread avocado on bread and top with cheese slice. Sprinkle on Spike and sesame seeds. Broil until cheese melts.

Makes wonderful hors d'oeuvres when sliced in triangles.

Apple-Jack Salad

5 apples
½ cup raisins
½ cup slivered almonds or ⅓ cup sunflower seeds
1 cup Monterey Jack cheese

Peel, core, and slice apples. Combine with raisins, almonds, and cubed chunks of Monterey Jack cheese.

Serve over lettuce as is or with your favorite dressing.

Sweet Cheese Spread

½ cup cottage or ricotta cheese
2 Tbs. chopped walnuts or pecans
2 Tbs. chopped dates

Mix together and spread over whole wheat bread or toast.

Yogurt

1 quart skim or whole milk
1 envelope skim milk powder (optional; fortifies and thickens)
2 Tbs. yogurt, room temperature

Heat milk until it almost reaches boiling point. (Use a pot that you can store and serve from.) Let it cool until you can put your finger in and count to ten (Lebanese method). Add yogurt (and skim milk powder). Stir in gently.

Cover pot. Wrap blanket completely around pot, or place pot on stove over pilot light, or place in oven (heat off). Above all, be sure it is away from draft. Leave overnight.

In morning, place in refrigerator.

Raita

This is the way yogurt is served in India. Since it has a cooling effect, raita goes well with curry dishes.

1 cup plain yogurt
1 cucumber, peeled and cubed
1 tsp. salt
½ tsp. powdered coriander
½ tsp. cumin powder
Combine all ingredients.

Mint Raita

1 cup yogurt
1 cucumber, peeled and cubed
1 Tbs. finely chopped mint leaves
Combine all ingredients.

Miso Yogurt Dip

2 scallions
2 Tbs. miso
2 Tbs. tahini
½ tsp. grated ginger
1 cup yogurt

Chop scallions, separating green from white part. Mix miso, tahini, ginger, and white part of scallions. Mix in yogurt. Garnish with green part of scallions.

Chill and serve with fresh vegetables.

Avocado Yogurt Dressing

1 avocado
½ cup yogurt
½ clove garlic, minced
1 tsp. lemon juice

Mash avocado and mix in other ingredients.

Yogurt Blue Cheese Sauce

1 cup yogurt
½ cup blue cheese
¼ cup olive oil
½ tsp. sea salt

Combine ingredients and blend until smooth. This is good on salads, as a dip, or as a sauce for beanburgers or felafel.

Chapter 11

Let Us
Be Fruitful

Fruits are too often taken for granted and not given the respect they deserve.

When traveling through India, we were served guava in such a way that we can still recall the taste. We were sitting in a circle with a group of Swamis on a lovely hilltop in Rishikesh, surrounded by the foothills of the Himalayas and overlooking the Ganges River. The air was filled with the scent of sandlewood and incense.

One of the sanyasins (spiritual seekers) came around and offered slices of guava, beautifully arranged on large, freshly cut and washed palm leaves placed on hand-carved sandlewood serving trays. There were two equal mounds of salt and pepper at the center of the tray. We each took a slice of guava, added a pinch of salt and pepper, bowed slightly in reverence to its Creator, and then slowly ate it. We were so conscious of eating that particular guava that we recall its taste to this day.

The secret of really enjoying a fruit is to eat the fruit while you are eating the fruit.

If that sounds redundant to you, stop and think of all the times you have eaten a fruit while having your mind on something else. I remember once eating a peach while being introduced to a pretty girl. When I finished eating the peach and the girl had left, I had no recollection of the taste of the peach I had eaten. All I remembered was the peach I was introduced to!

A similar incident occurred once while I was eating an apple. My mind was on some problem at the time I was eating it, and when the apple was finished, I had no sense of having eaten it and craved another.

Many people overeat for that reason. They are not conscious of the food they are eating while they are eating it, thus they get little or no satisfaction from it. They immediately crave more food and then do the same thing with that food.

One of the main reasons spiritual people say a prayer before eating food (some even before eating a fruit) is to draw full consciousness to the food they are about to eat and the purpose they are eating it for.

In the EST training, a seminar designed to raise the level of experience, and one from which Runa and I got tremendous value, we had a total experience of a strawberry. After a long period without a food break, we were directed to close our eyes and imagine a strawberry as tall as the room we were sitting in. We were then told to imagine ourselves climbing up the side of our giant strawberry and jumping down inside it. After the process, we were each given a strawberry and directed to eat it very slowly, being conscious of its texture, aroma, taste, and appearance. As with the guava, I can still vividly recall the taste of that particular strawberry.

Another way to get the full enjoyment from fruit is to serve it with attention and respect, rather than just grabbing it out of the refrigerator and gulping it down. One of our favorite forms of refreshment in Italy was ordering a peach in a restaurant; whether it was in a first-class restaurant or just a quick-order snack bar, the peach was carefully washed, chilled, and served on a plate with a knife and fork. Similarly, in Florence in the summertime we would cool off by stopping at the watermelon wagons in the streets, where we would be served a chilled slice of watermelon on a plate with a knife and fork.

BUYING AND SELECTING FRUIT

We buy fruits only in season and select those that are firm and ripe. Ideally, fruits should be left to ripen on the tree or vine. Unripened fruit should be kept at room temperature until soft. We find it best to buy bananas when they are green, however, as sometimes they are gassed by the shipper to induce ripeness. Bananas should be eaten only when they are fully ripe.

In selecting citrus fruits, we look for those with thin skins and heavy weight for maximum juice. Oranges are often colored to make them more eye-appealing; we look for the paler oranges with green on the rinds.

The only canned fruit we buy is pineapple packed in its own juice with no sugar added. Sugar should never be added to fruit and most canned fruits are loaded with it.

Out of season, we also buy frozen blueberries and strawberries. They are a good source of fruit sugars and help us curtail our desire for sweets.

Drying or dehydrating is an excellent way of preserving fruits and having them available all year round. We eat only fruits which are sun-dried and avoid fruits that are sulphur-dried and softened with preservatives. All it takes is soaking with a little water to bring dried fruits back to a soft, sweet taste. And the water will turn into delicious syrup. Try water-soaked dried apricots chilled with slivered almonds or on top of honey-sweetened vanilla ice cream.

Dried fruits are easy to store. Keep them in glass bottles in a cool, dry cupboard. You can soak them overnight by putting them in a bowl with just enough water to cover. They'll be ready to eat the following morning or you can put them in the refrigerator and they will keep for a few days.

With dried and fresh fruits on hand, you will never need to buy canned fruits for the sake of convenience.

Blender Smoothies

There are many delicious blender fruit drinks that you can make. Here are a few of our favorites:

2 cups pineapple juice/1 cup fresh strawberries/1 banana

1 cup fresh orange juice/1 cup fresh mango

1 cup pineapple juice/1 peach/1 cup cut mango

4 cups apple juice/1 cup fresh strawberries

In each case, simply blend and serve.

Most fruit salad recipes are poor combinations of acid and alkaline fruits. Try these simple combinations of compatible fruits and enjoy.

Tropical Treat

2 papayas
3 bananas
2 mangos
shredded coconut

Combine slices of fresh fruits. Top with shredded coconut.

Berry Treat

1 cup strawberries
1 cup raspberries
1 cup blueberries

Combine berries and serve with yogurt topping, or sprinkle with fructose, or just eat them the way they are.

Hot Blueberry Sauce

$\frac{1}{2}$ cup water
1 Tbs. arrowroot starch
pinch of sea salt
2 cups blueberries
2 Tbs. honey or maple syrup
1 tsp. lemon juice

Combine water, arrowroot, and salt in saucepan, and stir over low heat until thickened. Add blueberries, honey, and lemon juice and stir in.

Serve over pancakes, ice cream, yogurt.

Rainbow Salad

1 cup each of:
blueberries
avocado, diced
banana, sliced
mango or papaya, diced
strawberries, sliced

Arrange fruit in horizontal strips on a large serving dish. Follow the order as they are listed, according to the rainbow: blue, green, yellow, orange, red.

Oliver's Banana Split

Oliver made this himself one day and has since enjoyed serving it to his friends.

Cut unpeeled banana lengthwise. Mash banana in the peel. Put a little yogurt on top. Top with jam, wheat germ, and chopped nuts. Vary by using honey or date sugar in place of jam and adding coconut and sesame seeds.

Papaya Split

Cut whole papaya in half, remove seeds, and fill as in banana split above.

Avocado Split

Cut avocado in half, remove pit, and fill with yogurt and honey, topped with wheat germ and roasted sesame seeds. Or fill with cottage cheese, top with tahini and honey. Sprinkle wheat germ on top.

Yogi's Lunch

Arrange on table, bowls of any amount of the following:

large bowl of assorted fresh fruit: blueberries, sliced apples, pears, bananas, peaches, mangos, strawberries, etc.

one or more bowls of nuts: almonds, raw cashews, walnuts, pecans, sunflower seeds, pignolias

large bowl of yogurt

small bowl of raisins

small bowl of wheat germ

small bowl of tahini

small bowl of shredded coconut

dispenser filled with honey

With large serving spoon serve fruit on plate. Add nuts. With another large serving spoon, cover fruits and nuts with yogurt. Add a tablespoon each of raisins, wheat germ, and tahini. Sprinkle over a small spoonful of shredded coconut. Drip honey out of dispenser in a circular pattern over all. Place a strawberry in the center and *"bon appétit."*

Fruit and Dairy Lunch

Place a mound of cottage cheese in the center of a bed of lettuce. Surround with banana slices alternating with pitted dates. Spread around a small handful of pecans or walnuts. Spoon strawberry yogurt over the top. Sprinkle with pignolia nuts together with some wheat germ and honey.

Fruit Agar-Agar

Agar-agar is a tasteless sea vegetable that jells and can be used in place of animal gelatin or pectin. It is low in carbohydrate.

2 cups apple juice
1 cup water
pinch sea salt
1 Tbs. agar-agar
banana or other fruits

Bring liquids to a boil. Add salt and agar-agar. Stir until dissolved, then simmer for 15 minutes.

Rinse mold or bowl in cold water. Arrange fruits at bottom and pour liquid over it. Let set at room temperature (about 2 hours) and then put in refrigerator to chill.

Unmold, or serve from bowl.

Variation
Use boysenberry or other juices in place of apple.

Fruit Pudding

1 cup chopped figs
1 cup chopped dates
1 cup raisins
1 cup nut milk
1 Tbs. lemon juice

Blend thoroughly and serve in dessert cups. Sprinkle coconut shreds on top.

Variation
Add chopped nuts to blender for a chewier dessert.

136

Apple Butter

Apple butter is a delicious ingredient for spreads, desserts, candies, and yogurt. We usually buy ours in the health food store or health food section of supermarkets. Buy only the unsweetened kind, as it is sweet naturally and doesn't need honey or sugar. If you want to make your own, here is the simple recipe:

Put cooked apple sauce in a heavy pot (cast iron preferred). Cook over low heat for 2-3 hours, stirring often to prevent sticking. For added flavor you can add a couple of teaspoons of cinnamon, a teaspoon of cloves, juice of a lemon and a little honey.

Apricot Butter

2 cups dried, unsulphured apricots
2 cups water
juice of 1 lemon
½ cup honey
1 tsp. arrowroot (if desired)

Soak apricots in water overnight in closed glass container.

Put fruit along with soak water in blender with lemon juice. Put mixture in jar and add honey. Mix well. Thicken, if desired, by heating in saucepan with 1 teaspoon of arrowroot that has been dissolved in a little water.

Chapter 12

Juices Keep Our Juices Flowing

In our house, things *do not* go better with coke.

But they definitely do go better with carrot, apple, celery, parsley, spinach, watercress, pineapple, and grape juice.

People who wouldn't think of letting their children drink coffee give little, if any thought at all, to the fact that the colas they let them drink contain half the caffeine of the same amount of coffee.

Get your kids to stop opening soda pops and teach them to start cutting carrot tops. A juice-extracting machine is an investment that will pay high dividends in health and vitality for the whole family. When your children won't eat raw vegetables or salad, a glass of fresh, raw vegetable juice will ensure that they are getting a nutritious supply of vitamins and minerals.

Vegetable juices are builders and regenerators of the human body, providing a good supply of amino acids, minerals, salts, enzymes, and vitamins. These juices are digested and assimilated within 15 minutes after we drink them and are then used almost entirely in the nourishment and regeneration of the cells and tissues.

Raw carrot juice is one of the richest sources of vitamin A and is loaded with vitamins B, C, D, E, G, and K. It also contains a good supply of calcium, magnesium, iron, sodium, potassium, phosphorus, sulphur, silicon, and chlorine. Carrot juice is beneficial to nursing mothers as well as growing infants. In his book *Raw Vegetable Juices*, N. W. Walker says that one pint of carrot juice daily has more constructive body value than 25 pounds of calcium tablets.

Although we used to give Oliver and Jonathan cow's milk, we took them off it by gradually adding carrot juice to their milk until it was just pure carrot juice. Carrot juice and milk are a compatible combination and this mixture is a good way to introduce carrot juice to your children.

If your children have been drinking a lot of colas and soft drinks, there is a good chance they are "hooked" on either the caffeine or the sugar, so switch over gradually by decreasing the amount of soda while adding carrot and apple juice to the menu. This combination will help satisfy their sweet tooth while also cleansing the liver and pancreas. As they get accustomed to the apple and carrot juice, you can begin to add parsley, celery, watercress, and so on. Our favorite combination is carrot, apple, and celery juice.

We're very pleased that Oliver and Jonathan are starting off life so early with raw vegetable and fruit juices! It is sad to see mothers in supermarkets stocking up on sugary soft drinks for their children.

And it's interesting to note that we've never had to worry about Oliver or Jonathan drinking any dangerous chemicals out of a can. We feel that this is because they have no association that good things to drink come out of cans, having never seen us do it.

Most parents are aware of the dangers of leaving poisonous chemicals within reach of a child, but many don't realize the dangers of slow poisoning with colas and other soft drinks. Substances that can remove paint from an automobile, and some colas will do just that, are not the best liquids to be pouring into a child's body.

We make our own sodas by mixing apple or grape juice with spring water or with a sparkling mineral water. We also squeeze a lemon into a glass of mineral water and sweeten with a little fructose. There is a wide variety of juices available at health food stores and, while they are expensive, you can extend their use by diluting them with waters or herbal teas.

We've heard neighbors complain that they can't afford pure apple or grape juice and have to buy fruit punches. Yet it's easy to dilute the bottled juices and squeeze in some lemon for added flavor and vitamin C, thus getting more mileage out of real juice than from a can of artificial stuff.

Our favorite summertime drink is very inexpensive to make and is one of the most delicious and refreshing drinks you will find anywhere. It's our apple juice-spearmint tea drink and you'll find our recipe for it along with other drinks in the recipe section that follows.

Spring Water

We had been hearing about the hazards of drinking tap water for so long that we finally decided to keep a 5-gallon bottle of spring water in our kitchen. A handy pump that fits on the bottle is available at some health food stores. We exchange the empty bottles for refills at the store, but you may be able to get delivery in your area. At first we used spring water only for drinking, but now we use it for cooking as well. We try to save the cooking water and use it as a base for soup the next day, getting the benefit of the water and all the vitamins left behind from the vegetables.

Tap filters and water purifiers are somewhat helpful in removing many of the harmful contaminants, but if you can afford it, you would do much better with spring water.

The next time you raise a glass saying "Here's to your health," look at what you're about to drink to see if it really is.

Apple Spearmint Tea

1 quart water
1 handful dried spearmint or peppermint leaves
1 quart apple juice
1 lemon

Put water and leaves in pot. Heat until boiling. Turn off heat and let steep for 3 to 5 minutes. Strain into 2-quart container, and add apple juice. Squeeze juice of ½ lemon and add to tea. Cut other half of lemon in slices and add. Chill and serve.

In summer, we pick fresh spearmint leaves and add a few to the container.

Variations

Instead of spearmint use camomile, papaya mint, alfalfa mint, Red Zinger, or other herb teas.

Iced Apple-Grape-Spearmint Tea

1 quart water
1 handful dried spearmint leaves
½ quart apple juice or cider
½ quart grape juice
juice of 2 lemons

With water and leaves, make spearmint tea as in the preceding recipe. Add juices.

Try serving this in a punch bowl with slices of lemon. You can also add some sparkling spring water for extra zing.

142

Mu Tea and Apple Juice

Mu tea is a delicious blend of 16 medicinal plants, herbs, and seeds, including ginseng root. It can be purchased at most health food stores. Follow brewing instructions on the package and add an equal amount of apple juice. Serve either hot, at room temperature, or chilled.

Hot Cider

Heat cider. Add orange slices and cinnamon sticks.

Chapter 13

Snacks Can be Healthful

A SURVIVAL MANUAL FOR PARENTS WITH GROWING CHILDREN

Raising children on a diet of whole, natural foods is a worthwhile, but, let's face it, difficult path to tread.

What do you do, for example, when the ice cream truck is ringing its bell on your street and all the neighborhood kids are licking ice cream pops and ice sticks?

Or when your child's best friend is having a birthday party filled to the brim with ice cream, cake, candy, and colas?

Or when you have to find a snack for your child's lunch box to compete with his or her classmates' chocolate marshmallow cupcake?

Or when you're leaving the supermarket with your child and have to run the gauntlet of bubble gum and candy machines that line the exit?

Or when you're making a deposit at the bank and the teller suddenly whips out a lollipop colored with red dye?

There *are* times when we wonder, "Is it really worth all this trouble?" But once making a commitment to go the natural route, it is almost impossible to turn back to the world of junk foods. For "the mind expanded by a new idea can never return to its original dimension."

Daily threats to your child's health via the lure of junk foods can be looked at as opportunities to use your ingenuity. If you put your mind to it, you can find and create healthful, nutritious snacks to replace the detrimental ones that now flood the commercial marketplace.

Our children actually prefer our own ice pops (made by freezing pure fruit juices in a Tupperware ice pop mold) to those made of sugar and artificial syrup. And our pure and delicious pops cost a fraction of the price you pay for the junky ones. In place of ice cream pops, we offer homemade yogurt pops (recipes given in this chapter).

There are three ways we handle the problem of sending our children to birthday parties. (1). We make a decision not to send them. (2). We provide the other parents with healthful treats for our children (only if we know they won't be insulted). (3). We let them go, but first fill them up with lots of healthful food and *never* let them go with a full appetite.

It's very important to communicate to the child about what you are doing and why you are doing it. We don't just say "no" to Oliver and Jonathan. We tell them why certain foods are not good for their bodies and encourage them to develop their own control over eating them. One day Oliver came home from a friend's birthday party and said: "Mommy, I have something to tell you that you won't like, but then I have something to tell you that you will like. First the bad news: I had some birthday cake at Adam's party. Now the good news: I didn't eat the icing."

Jonathan is also developing self-control and awareness. He recently said, "May I have a piece of candy?" We said, "No, Jonathan, it's not good for your body. Have a carrot

146

instead." Jonathan replied, "Well, can I have just a little piece for my tongue, even if my body doesn't like it?"

Snacks can be a great way to give your children high-protein and nutritious foods instead of the harmful sugars, carbohydrates, and artificial ingredients that constitute most junk food snacks. Chocolate, regarded as being highly detrimental by most nutritionists, can be replaced by carob, one of nature's oldest health foods. Sugar, the worst enemy, can be replaced by honey, maple syrup, date sugar, molasses, or fructose. We are gradually trying to wean our children away from sweets altogether. Their sweet tooth can often be satisfied with fruits or dried fruits.

When their friends are nibbling on pretzels and potato chips, Oliver and Jonathan have a bag of roasted soy nuts, rice cakes, or nuts and raisins. With a little practice and planning you too can provide your children with snacks that are really nutritious.

Homemade Potato Chips

Preheat oven to 450°.

Peel potatoes and cut in half. Using a potato peeler, cut thin slices from the flat surface.

Spread slices out on an oiled cookie sheet. Brush the potatoes with oil and bake for 10 minutes or until brown. Add sea salt to taste.

Tahini Candy Roll

Prepare Tahini Yogurt (see Chapter 8), but use less yogurt and add high-protein powder or soya powder to the mixture. Shape into balls or logs and roll in wheat germ and coconut. Refrigerate or freeze. Delicious.

147

Sesame Oatmeal Cookies

⅓ cup honey
½ cup oil
1 egg, beaten
¼ cup milk
1 cup whole wheat flour
1¼ cups oatmeal
⅓ cup soy flour
¼ tsp. salt
1 tsp. ground cinnamon
¾ cup sesame seeds
½ cup raisins or chopped dates

Preheat oven to 375°.

Blend together honey, oil, egg, and milk. Stir in remaining ingredients. Mixture should be stiff. Thin with milk or thicken with flour as necessary.

Drop batter by tablespoons onto oiled cookie sheet and bake for 10 to 15 minutes.

Dried Fruit and Nut Balls

1 cup dates
1 cup raisins
½ cup coconut shreds
1 cup wheat germ
1 cup chopped sunflower seeds
1 cup sun-dried figs
¼ cup coconut shreds, to roll

Finely chop or grind all but the last ingredient. Roll into balls or logs, adding honey, if you prefer, for added consistency. Roll balls in coconut and refrigerate.

Variations

Use chopped pecans, walnuts, and other nuts in place of or in combination with sunflower seeds.

Instead of coconut, roll in toasted sesame seeds.

Granola Bars

½ cup peanut butter
¼ cup honey
2 Tbs. softened butter
1 tsp. vanilla
2 cups Homemade Granola (see Chapter 3)

Preheat oven to 350°.

Combine peanut butter, honey, butter, and vanilla in mixing bowl. Mix in granola.

Spread evenly in oiled 9-inch square pan. Bake for 10 minutes. Cut squares and let cool.

Granola Apple Betty

2 cups Homemade Granola (see Chapter 3)
½ cup soft butter
¼ cup honey
½ tsp. cinnamon
2½ cups sliced apples

Preheat oven to 350°.

Combine 1 cup of granola (reserving 1 cup) with butter, honey, and cinnamon. Spread mixture on bottom of 9-inch square baking pan. Place apples over crumbs. Sprinkle the rest of granola over top.

Bake for 25 to 30 minutes. Top with honey ice cream if you like.

Variations

Add ¼ cup coconut to mixture.

Use other fresh fruit in place of apples.

Granola Cookies

½ cup butter
4 Tbs. honey
1 egg
1 tsp. vanilla
¾ cup whole wheat pastry flour
½ tsp. baking soda
½ tsp. sea salt
¾ tsp. cinnamon
1½ cups Homemade Granola (see Chapter 3)
½ cup raisins (optional)
½ cup chopped nuts (optional)
Preheat oven to 350°.

Cream butter, honey, egg, and vanilla. Mix together flour, soda, salt, and cinnamon and add to butter mixture, stirring until smooth. Stir in granola, raisins, and nuts.

Drop by spoon onto ungreased baking sheet. Bake for 10 to 15 minutes.

Homemade Natural Crackerjacks

⅓ cup honey
⅓ cup melted butter or safflower oil
2 quarts popped popcorn
¾ cup raw peanuts (or other nuts, chopped)
Preheat oven to 350°.

Blend honey and butter or oil together in a heated saucepan. Mix popcorn and nuts and pour the honey-butter mixture over it. Mix well and spread on a cookie sheet in a thin layer. Bake for 15 minutes or until crisp.

Yogurt Sherbet and Pops

1½ cups yogurt
1 small can frozen concentrated fruit juice
2 tsp. vanilla (optional)
1 banana, ripe
Combine all ingredients. Mix well and put in tray or ice pop molds in freezer.

Carob Brownies

⅔ cups whole wheat flour
½ tsp. baking powder
¼ tsp. salt
4 Tbs. carob powder
⅓ cup vegetable oil
½ cup honey
½ cup peanut butter
3 eggs
½ cup chopped nuts
1 tsp. vanilla
Preheat oven to 350°.
    Combine flour, baking powder, and salt. Add carob to oil.
    Add honey and peanut butter to eggs. Beat well. Blend in carob mixture. Add flour and blend. Add nuts and vanilla and mix.
    Spread in an oiled 8 by 8 by 9 inch pan. Bake for 25 minutes. Let cool in pan and cut in squares.

Granola Candy

Add honey and coconut to Homemade Granola (see Chapter 3) until it sticks together. Form into balls, wrap in waxed paper, and refrigerate.

Chapter 14

Born Free and Natural

The condition of the mother's body, not only during pregnancy, but before it as well, can have a lot to do with the formation of the child. And the condition of the father's body can also be an influence. If you are planning to have a child in the near future, the time to start thinking about its health and nutrition is now, by seeing that your own body gets a diet of whole, natural foods, a good amount of exercise, pure water, and fresh air.

As soon as a woman learns she is pregnant, she should start to cleanse the inside of her body with herbs. Herbs help to cleanse the intestinal walls, thus contributing toward greater absorption and assimilation of vitamins from the food you eat. Herbs are also helpful for other organs of the body, such as the kidney, liver, pancreas, etc. This chapter contains several herb tea recipes. Cleansing herbs are also available in capsule and tablet form at many health food stores.

Herb teas also make good substitutes for coffee. It is advisable not to have too much coffee during pregnancy, as caffeine depletes the body of its much-needed iron and B vitamins. Some herb teas are also excellent remedies for nausea or "morning sickness."

In addition to preparing your body for pregnancy, you should also prepare your mind, by making it calm. Swami Satchidananda has said that the state of the mother's mind can be a determining factor on the type of child she has. In many communities in India, as soon as the woman learns she is pregnant, she is sent off to stay with her mother or mother-in-law, and everything is done to see that she enjoys a peaceful surrounding. She is treated like a goddess.

We needn't go so far in America, but there are certain measures that can be taken—such as avoiding violence in books, movies, and television. Too much television exposure of *any* kind can build up the total of harmful radiation and should be kept to a minimum during pregnancy.

Cigarette smoking is another habit that is detrimental during pregnancy. It has been proven over and over again that cigarette smoking retards the growth of the fetus. You'll find it's easier to give up cigarette smoking when you also give up coffee and meat. Swamiji says the three "INE" sisters like to travel together: NicotINE, caffeINE, and purINE. So give up one and the others may join her.

Replace your cigarette smoking with deep breathing exercises. Fresh oxygen will fill the lungs and replace the urge for the artificial sensation of nicotine. Every time you have an urge for a cigarette, do some deep rapid breathing through the nostrils. Feel the oxygen fill your entire lungs and send fresh life into your bloodstream. Try to make this a daily habit —as soon as you wake up, during the day, and before you go to sleep. It will help build up the hemoglobin in your blood and you won't have to worry about anemia. It will also help calm the mind, especially if followed by meditation.

With proper exercise, avoidance of bad habits, a good, nutritional diet, and the elimination of refined, processed foods, pregnancy can truly be one of the most beautiful experiences of a woman's life. Birth can also be a beautiful, conscious experience, through natural childbirth. For the child, it provides the opportunity to enter life without drugs.

Teas for Morning Sickness
Peach leaves, peppermint, spearmint, red raspberry, golden-seal.

Teas to Promote Easy Childbirth
Spikenard tea is an old Indian remedy that promotes an easy childbirth. Take it alone or mix with red raspberry leaves. Drink about a cup a day during pregnancy. Other herbs that are known to be effective are black cohosh and blue cohosh, and lobelia, which is calming to the nerves.

Beverages for Nursing Mothers
Steep or boil fennel seed (about a tablespoon) in a cup of barley water. Strain and squeeze in a few drops of fresh lemon juice.

Ways to Increase Mother's Milk Supply
Eat whole grains, especially oats, millet, corn, and barley.
Drink oatmeal water and barley water.
Eat a lot of alfalfa sprouts.
Drink a lot of clover tea.
Drink fresh carrot, celery, and parsley juice.
Drink lots of spring water.

Oatmeal Water
Put two large tablespoons of oats in a quart of water and simmer for a half an hour. Then beat up with an egg beater and strain through a fine sieve. Add a little more oatmeal if you want it thicker.

Instead of water, you can simmer the oats in Soy Milk (see Chapter 4) for added nutritional value. Drink while it's warm to increase the flow of milk. It also makes an excellent drink for a baby.

BABY'S FIRST FOOD WILL BE HIS BEST: NURSING

There is no perfect replacement for mother's milk, and no other time in life will a human being be provided with food more nourishing.

Unless it is physically impossible, every mother-to-be should consider nursing her child. We have known some mothers who chose formulas simply for their own convenience, so they would be able to go away for a tennis or ski weekend and leave the baby with the nurse. If you are not prepared to breast-feed your baby, it's best to avoid having a child. In addition to the close physical contact with your baby, you will also be missing one of nature's ways of keeping your body healthy; the La Leche League (an information center for nursing mothers) reports that there is a significantly lower rate of breast cancer among women who have nursed their babies.

The baby also will benefit from being breast-fed. Quantitative studies have proved that breast-fed babies are more resistant to colds, coughs, allergies, and diseases than bottle-fed babies, since mother's milk provides natural antibodies.

Many nutritionists believe it is not good or natural to give cow's milk to a baby, especially for the first nine months. They point out that the cassein content in cow's milk is far out of proportion for human needs. Cassein is what helps build the bone structure of the animal necessary to carry its body weight. In a cow's milk, the cassein content is 300 times more than it is in mother's milk. It is intended to grow a calf into a cow weighing about three-quarters of a ton. Cow's milk is intended to double the weight of the calf in the period of six to eight weeks. A human baby requires six to seven months to double its body weight.

Also, human milk is abundant in phosphorus, as opposed to the great amounts of calcium in cow's milk. Phosphorus is very important for brain growth and development. The human baby develops its brains first, whereas the animal develops its bone structure first.

As a healthy alternative to cow's milk, we offer the following formulas.

Natural Formulas

These natural food formulas are a healthy alternative to cow's milk and are suited for babies that have been weaned from the breast. Prepare all formulas in the blender at high speed for 3 minutes and strain through a fine strainer or cheesecloth.

Formula No. 1
1 cup almonds
¼ cup sesame seeds
1 quart spring water
2 Tbs. uncooked honey or blackstrap molasses
Follow instructions above.

Formula No. 2
½ cup almonds
½ cup cashews
¼ cup raisins
1 Tbs. honey
1 quart spring water
Follow instructions above.

Formula No. 3
½ cup almonds
½ cup coconut
4 chopped dates
1 quart water (or in combination with fresh coconut milk)
Follow instructions above.

Formula No. 4

1 quart Soy Milk (see Chapter 4)

2 Tbs. sesame or sunflower seeds

1 Tbs. honey or molasses

Follow instructions above.

HELPING YOUR BABY BECOME A SOLID CITIZEN: WEANING

Our two children were nursed for close to a year and we know of many other people who have done it much longer. We first introduced foods by way of freshly extracted fruit and vegetable juices, diluted with spring water. Then we gradually offered mashed ripe fruit such as banana and avocado.

At the time we introduced vegetables to our baby, we steamed them for our own dinner and put the baby's portion in the blender, so as to avoid making separate meals. We have never used commercial baby food. If we expected to be out for the day, we would prepare the baby's food, put it in a wide-mouthed thermos, and take it along.

Cereals and other starches should not be served to the child until he or she is at least 10 months old and has developed the enzyme ptyalin, which aids in the digestion of starch.

It is helpful to have a nut grinder or coffee mill, so that you can finely grind nuts, seeds, and cereals to feed the baby. Millet is one of the most nutritious cereals for a baby and is best prepared by grinding it down first and then cooking it (recipe is given in this chapter).

If you have doubts about raising a child as a vegetarian, let us reassure you that a baby can get all the protein and nutrition he or she needs from vegetarian foods and you need not resort to meat for the first two years. Once the child fully develops the teeth and digestive organs, then you can allow him or her the choice of eating meat if you so prefer. But if you feed the baby the food that is mentioned in this book, be forewarned. You may have an incurable vegetarian on your hands!

We do not firmly believe that everybody should be vegetarians. Certain body types and blood types may crave and require meat. But we do believe everybody should be given a clear choice. So please, don't rush it. Let your baby grow his full set of teeth and let him decide what *he's* going to chew with them.

Banana Blendies for Baby
Ripe bananas are a perfect food for babies. Their peels protect them from sprays, dust, and bacteria. They help regulate the babies' digestive functions. Mash and serve alone or blend in fruits such as avocado, peaches, pears, papaya, mango, etc.

Baby's Granola
Using our Homemade Granola recipe (see Chapter 3), grind granola fine in a grain or coffee mill and mix with warm Cashew Milk, Almond Milk (see Chapter 8), or Soy Milk (see Chapter 4). Or add the milk to the granola in a blender, and blend until smooth.

Baby's Millet
We consider millet one of the best cereals for babies as well as adults. First grind millet and store in a jar. Sprinkle 4 tablespoons of millet in a cup of boiling water. Stir and cook over low heat for 15 minutes.

Or cook baby's millet along with your own and put it in the blender with spring water, milk, nut milk (see Chapter 8), or Soy Milk (see Chapter 4). Add a little honey and serve.

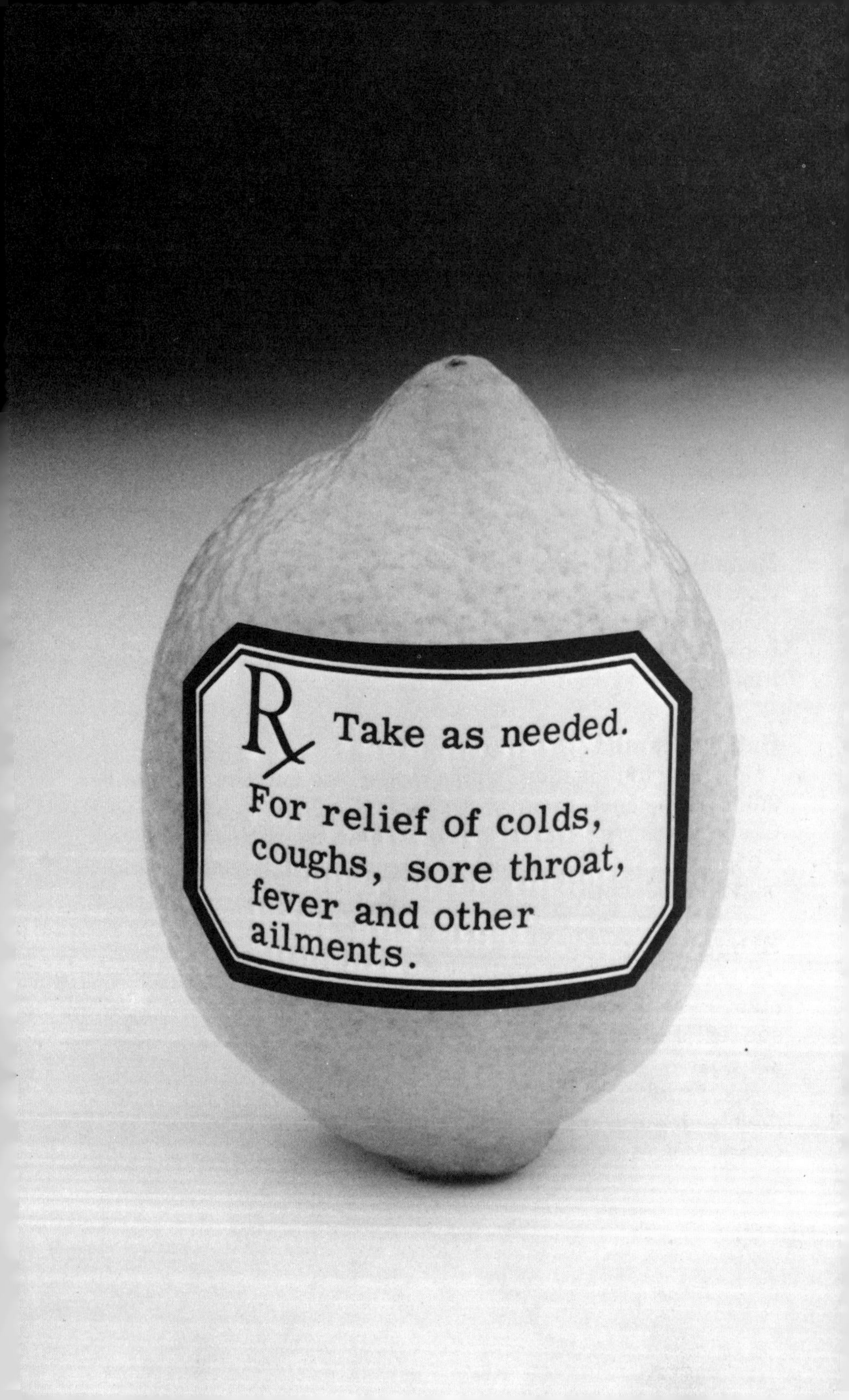
Rx Take as needed.
For relief of colds, coughs, sore throat, fever and other ailments.

Chapter 15

How to Use Your Kitchen Cabinet Instead of a Medicine Cabinet

Right within your own kitchen cabinets are foods and herbs that can help relieve many physical ailments. They are so readily available that many people snub their noses when they hear of their curative abilities, write them off as "old folk remedies," and put their full faith into the little plastic bottles of pills that come from their pharmacist.

To attribute amazing curative qualities to a lemon may be a little difficult for the medicine-oriented public to accept. But people were paying as much as 6,000 lira for a lemon during a recent cholera epidemic in Naples.

Granted, there are times when medicines can be life-saving, but we should first seek to understand the nature of an illness and find out what natural substances can be used to clear it up before running to the medicine cabinet.

Once we start to learn about the nature of illness and the effects herbs and medicinal plants can have, we can approach the healing process from a completely different point of view and de-program ourselves from all the fear propaganda we have been exposed to since childhood. Fortunately, herbs are beginning to get some of the respect by medical authorities in this country as they have received in European countries such as Germany and Switzerland.

Herbs are available in many health food stores and by mail order. Consult the periodicals listed in our bibliography, for more information on herbs.

There are many remedies with food and herbs that you can read about in the book *Back to Eden* by Jethro Kloss— considered to be the bible of herbal healing. We keep it handy and consult it frequently. Some of the herbs listed may not be readily available to you at the time you discover you need them, but there are common food remedies also, for everything from mumps to measles.

When we have a sore throat or cough we make a mixture of lemon juice and honey or apple cider vinegar and honey as an alternative to cough syrup or lozenges.

When the boys were teething, we applied a mixture of honey and ground cloves. For colic, we have had success with catnip and camomile tea and a wonderful bottle of dill water from India.

When our head gets stuffed up we use, as a decongestant, peppermint or spearmint leaves steeped in a pot of boiling water; wrap a towel around our head and pot and create an herbal sauna.

If a natural recovery from illness, without negative side effects is your cup of tea, try an herbal cup of tea. Following are a few sample herbal formulas.

Fever Tea
Fever is nature's way of burning up impurities. It is one of the

162

most wrongly feared and misunderstood functions of the human body. Since childhood, we have been taught to fear fever and do everything within our power to bring it down to normal. For years, aspirin commercials have been drumming that message into our heads.

But how many of us stop to think about what fever actually is and what its purpose is. Recently a group of scientists found that when the body raises its temperature it activates certain antibodies that help fight the invasion of bacteria and germs. And they advised that it is detrimental to take aspirin to lower the fever as you are interfering with the normal functioning of your body's chemistry.

In European health clinics they even induce fever to heal acute illnesses and diseases. So perhaps when fever comes, we should welcome it. It is an ally to our body and not a foe.

At the onset of fever it is best to eliminate all solid foods and drink lots of liquids. Lemon juice and water will help cleanse the body. Herbs for fever include: camomile, peppermint, spearmint, raspberry leaves, elderberry blossoms, sage, yarrow, catnip, parsley, sarsaparilla and wild cherry bark.

Headache Tea

Headache is a danger signal. When a certain organ or part of the body is not functioning normally, nature gives a warning. Therefore it is unwise to resort to aspirins or other pain-relieving drugs. You may dull the pain, but the source of trouble is still there and eventually may result in greater disturbances.

Try a cup of strong, hot peppermint tea, and lie down and relax. Other herbs that are effective for headaches are catnip, blue skullcap, valerian, and nerve root.

Many headaches originate in the colon. Drink plenty of water and lemon juice.

Headaches are often the result of misaligned vertebrae. Have your spine checked by a competent specialist.

Cold and Flu Teas

We regard a cold as nature's way of eliminating toxins. The quicker you open the channels of elimination, the quicker you will get over the cold. Eliminate all dairy products (as they are mucus-forming), as well as concentrated starches and carbohydrates.

Effective teas are alfalfa, peppermint and camomile. Lemon juice and water is an effective cleanser. Carrot and spinach juice is another. In *Folk Medicine*, D. C. Jarvis says it is possible to induce a quick recovery from a cold by changing the urine from alkaline to acid by taking 2 teaspoons of honey and 2 teaspoons of cider vinegar in a glass of water.

Sore Throat

Gargle with 2 tablespoons of cider vinegar in a glass of hot water to which a pinch of salt and of cayenne have been added.

Make a tea from horehound, slippery elm bark, licorice root, and lemon juice. Add honey to make an effective cough syrup and sore throat reliever.

Colic and Teething Tea

Make a weak, warm tea from any one or more of the following herbs: catnip, camomile, elder flowers, peppermint, or fennel seed.

Cough Control Tea

To one pint of boiling water, add a pinch of cayenne, a slice of lemon, 3 tablespoons of honey, and 1 ounce of shredded slippery elm bark. Steep for ½ hour. Take frequently in small doses. This tea is also helpful for whooping cough.

Stomachache Tea

Slippery elm bark is an excellent demulcent that has a soothing effect on the stomach and intestines by neutralizing stomach acids. Various herb teas that have a soothing effect on the stomach are wild cherry bark, caraway seed, goldenseal, sarsaparilla, camomile, peppermint, and papaya tea.

Sinus Teas

A cause of sinus congestion is an over consumption of mucus- and acid-forming foods. Milk, meat, cheese, and cereals are acid-forming, and should be replaced with foods that have an alkaline reaction, such as fruits and vegetables. Milk should be replaced by soymilk, and freshly extracted juices; carrot, celery, etc. Make a tea of one or a combination of the following herbs: goldenseal, plantain, elderberry, fennel seed, hops, yellow dock, burdock root, and red clover blossoms.

Pain Tea

As an alternative to aspirin, and its many dangerous side effects, one can get relief from pain with herb teas. Pain is greatly exaggerated when there is a lack of phosphorus and potassium, which can be found in the following herbs: camomile, plantain, stinging nettle, dandelion, comfrey, fennel seed, caraway seed, marigold flowers, and licorice root.

Nerve Tea

A combination of camomile and peppermint can have a soothing effect on the nerves and also help relieve a nervous headache. Other herbs that are effective in soothing the nerves are catnip, valerian, skullcap, motherwort, hops, garden sage, and celery seeds. Herbs such as these contain the minerals potassium, sodium, calcium, magnesium, iron, and phosphorus and have an alkaline reaction.

Chapter 16

Food for Thought

Most people go through life unaware of the magnificent machinery of their own bodies and the effect food has on it. When they get sick, when they end up with a malfunctioning organ, gallstones, or kidney stones, or when they go through their later years with chronic constipation, they think of it as a misfortune that befell them out of the blue, an infliction that it was their bad luck to get.

They fail first to acknowledge that sometimes they were the cause of their own suffering, and then to take positive steps to overcome their condition by changing their lifestyles and eating habits. Many just go on repeating their old patterns.

In his marvelous book, *Natural Diet for Folks That Eat: Cookin' with Mother Nature*, Dick Gregory gives an outstanding illustration of people's regard for their body in the chapter called "The Body Owner's Manual":

The average person has no idea of the location of the organs, glands, vessels, nerves, arteries and other components of the body, to say nothing of a lack of knowledge of their function. And that internal ignorance is probably the best explanation for the kind of "food" most people shove into their bodies.

It is characteristic of the American dream for folks to work very hard to earn enough money or credit to surround themselves with pieces of machinery—a television set, a refrigerator, a dishwasher, a stereo, a clothes washer and dryer, and of course an automobile. But before they've earned a penny, Mother Nature has provided them with the finest mechanism imaginable—their own body. Yet most people appreciate this marvelous piece of equipment the least.

The tragic truth is that most folks treat their automobiles better than their own bodies. If it were definitely proved that smoking cigarettes in an automobile will instantly corrode the engine, every smoker would quit smoking in his car! No automobile owner would pour refined sugar into the gas tank, or stuff a steak in the carburetor, or shove wet, soggy white bread into the radiator. Automobile owners would never do such things because they know it would damage their precious machines.

Also, automobile owners are constantly in search of the best possible fuel for their cars. They are careful to change the oil regularly and see that the car is periodically lubricated. They check the owner's manual provided by the manufacturer of their cars to see that they are treating their machine correctly. Yet the car owner will park his automobile, run into a luncheonette and wreak havoc upon his personal machine.

Dick Gregory discusses all the parts of the body in the "Body Owner's Manual." We think every living person should have such a manual. We urge you to get this book; it is one of the best health food books on the market, and thoroughly enjoyable to read.

168

It is unfortunate that the most important information needed for health and well-being is neglected in our education. As the parents of two small children starting elementary school, we are suddenly being made aware of this large hole in our educational system. Runa has been visiting the classrooms and demonstrating how carrot juice is made and how good it is for you while telling the children about how their bodies work and how food affects it. Most teachers know very little of this fundamental knowledge. More emphasis is placed on the year Columbus discovered America than on the location and function of the colon.

I must have been over twenty years old before I ever heard the word *thyroid gland* let alone know its function. The other day Jonathan said: "Mommy, could I have some kelp on my vegetables. For my thyroid gland!" He may not understand what it is, but he has heard us mention it and he repeated it. We try to explain to our children as much as we can about the effect certain foods have on the body.

DISEASE IS THE ABSENCE OF EASE

Scientists are working night and day to find a cure for the many diseases and illnesses that inflict humanity. The best cure for disease and illness we know of is to watch your intake and prevent your body from ever getting sick. We believe that an ounce of prevention is worth a pound of cure.

As our yoga teacher Swami Satchidananda points out: "You even say you *caught* a cold. The cold was out there passing by and you *caught* it! So why catch it? Just let it go instead."

Letting it go, however, means having a body and mind that are at ease. "If you have ease," Swamiji says, "there can never be dis-ease. Disease is merely the absence of ease."

That is the main reason yoga practitioners lean toward a vegetarian diet. They find that vegetarian foods are best suited to keep the mind and body at ease or in a *satwic* state, as referred to in Sanskrit. But even in a vegetarian diet one has to learn to eat properly. We have met many vegetarians who did not reflect an image of health, well-being and tranquility. They ate lots of refined starches, too much dairy, overcooked vegetables, candy, ice cream, and other sweets.

Not only diet, but exercise also is very important in keeping the body fit and resistant to illness. Yoga exercises are most helpful in keeping the body at ease. They help to tone up the glands, muscles, organs, spine, and all the nerve centers. The yoga "asanas" do not cause strain as do many other exercises. They are done very gently, with grace and ease, thereby relaxing the entire body and allowing it to release stored tensions.

Yoga is the easiest exercise to practice: you need no special outfit, no equipment, and no special place to do it. All you need is a floor and a towel or blanket. At the Integral Yoga Institute, you can start a beginner's class at any time. You don't have to sign up for a course and the contribution is generally around $2.00 a class. There are quite a few Institutes around the country. Look in your phone directory to see if there is one where you live.

If you wish to start yoga on your own the book we recommend is *Integral Yoga-Hatha* by Swami Satchidananda. It is a clear, and easy-to-follow book on yogas asanas. It's published by Holt, Rinehart and Winston in paperback.

If you have heard about yoga and seen it demonstrated on television, but haven't as yet tried it, don't keep putting it off. Make it your intention to do it tomorrow. Get up 15 minutes earlier in the morning or, if that's not convenient, take some time in the middle of the day or before dinner and start practicing. You'll have to be persistent at first; your mind is going to come up with all sorts of excuses for not doing it. But once you set a pattern and stick to it, your day will feel incomplete without it. And you will have a feeling of well-being that you will not want to lose.

Once you are involved, you can also involve your children. In addition to strengthening their bodies, it will help to discipline their minds. At the end of the exercise session you can have a period of meditation. Start with one minute. Sit on the floor in a comfortable, cross-legged position. See that your spine is erect. Close your eyes and watch your breath. Watch it go in. Watch it go out. In. Out. In. Out. You can gradually build up the time. A mantra is most helpful in keeping the mind focused on one point in meditation. A mantra is a sound formula, the vibration of which can tune your mind to a cosmic wavelength and a state of peace and tranquility. They are given to the student by a spiritual master or an organization. Until you are given one you can use the words Om, Shalom, or Amen. Just keep repeating it over and over and focus your mind on it. Very soon, your mind will stop running here and there and come to the center, where you will find peace and tranquility.

As the body affects the mind, the mind also affects the body. Many physical ailments can be relieved simply by making the mind calm and at ease.

THE POWER THAT MADE THE BODY CAN HEAL THE BODY

When we speak with pride of our children's excellent health and of how easily they overcome illnesses, it is not them we are praising. Rather, it is the miracle and wisdom of the human body that we are in awe and admiration of. And we are best able to witness its ability when we don't interfere with its natural healing processes. At best, all we can expect to do is to assist it in its work.

We believe medical doctors are very valuable in the areas of emergency treatment and first aid. But they often know little about nutrition and, in many cases, follow the advice and advertisements of the pharmaceutical companies.

As Paavo Airola points out in his book *Are You Confused?* most doctors look upon their profession as a business and are not interested in biological medicine. It is a time-consuming and tedious job to try to discover the initial causative factors of ill health of each patient, then to convince and instruct him or her in necessary changes in environment, diet, living habits, and so on, which will help to rebuild and strengthen the patient's health. It is much faster to write a prescription for a drug which will temporarily suppress the unwanted symptoms and make the patient feel that he or she has really been helped . . .

An alternative type of doctor we have discovered recently is the naturopath. Naturopaths use healing and diagnostic methods including chiropractic, acupuncture, shiatsu, reflexology, iridology, colonic irrigation, herbalology, diet, and vitamins.

The naturopath uses treatments that are directed at correcting the underlying causes of disease, strengthening the patient's resistance and creating the most favorable conditions for the body's own healing process to take place.

This is in direct opposition to the conventional approach, which treats a specific symptom with a drug or other remedy without taking into consideration the patient's total condition of health. While a drug is alleviating the symptom of one illness, it may be causing an imbalance in the body resulting in the degeneration of another organ. It is an unfortunate fact that there are a rapidly increasing number of "iatrogenic" diseases, which are diseases caused by doctors or their prescriptions.

The naturopathic doctor, or the "doctor of biological medicine," will avail himself or herself of all the ancient and modern arts of examination and healing, recognizing that no doctor or remedy can cure disease, but that disease can be cured only by the body's own healing activity.

Holistic health seminars and health expositions are cropping up all over the country. They provide an excellent opportunity for exposure to all the natural methods that are being made available.

If you would like to stay abreast of all these events and read articles about the alternative, natural approaches to health, nutrition and mental awareness, there are quite a few new "alternative lifestyle" magazines, such as the *East West Journal, The New Age Journal, The New Sun,* and *Well-Being.* Consult our bibliography for a listing.

We feel fortunate to be living in such an extraordinary, awakening age, when all the ancient and modern methods of natural healing are coming to the forefront. Thomas Edison's prediction is indeed coming true: "The Doctor of the future will give no medicine (drugs); but will offer his patients care of the human frame, advice regarding diet, correction of the *cause* of human illness rather than the temporary relief of symptoms."

EATING WITH GRACE

We hope that this book will give you more of an awareness of the enormous variety of vegetarian foods, and that it will be more difficult after reading it for you to think of a vegetarian diet as merely "rabbit food."

And we have barely scratched the surface. There is still a tremendous variety of foods and an infinite amount of recipes that we haven't even touched on. We have shared only a handful of the ones we thought to be the most nutritious and practical.

At first we experimented with many, many recipes. Now, however, we are experiencing a great joy and satisfaction from eating the same basic foods. We no longer feel compelled to put on a great show for our senses. Rather than awakening the senses, highly seasoned meals tend to deaden them to basic, natural tastes. One discovers this after staying away from sugar for a while. You start to taste things you have never tasted before.

There's nothing wrong with being a gourmet, as long as you don't overdo it. But we suggest becoming a gourmet of life instead. Food is the fuel that keeps our body and mind working. Let us, therefore, eat to live and not live to eat.

Each moment is a brand new experience of life, so eat each mouthful of food as though you are eating it for the very first time. Detach yourself from your past memories of food.

Rather than eating as soon as food is put down in front of you, pause a while to acknowledge where it came from and to be conscious of the life-giving energy it is giving you and that "the body is the temple of the spirit." When you take the time to do this, you will find yourself enjoying each mouthful of food much more and eating only the food that is going to support you physically, mentally and spiritually.

We have ended our book with a beautiful Yogic prayer for before meals. It should not be looked at as a religious observance. Anyone can say it, regardless of faith. It is pronounced in the original Sanskrit at the Integral Yoga Institutes and the Satchidananda Ashram; it is quite an experience to sit down for a meal at an Integral Yoga Retreat with a thousand people, say the prayer, and then eat in total silence.

You can use this prayer, or say one from your own religion, or you can even make one up yourself. In Sweden, they say, "Gode Gud Valsingna maten, Amen," "Dear God, bless this food."

Yoga Prayer Before Meals

Mother Nature, who comes to our table as food,
Endlessly bountiful, benefactor of all:
Grant us health and strength, wisdom and dispassion.

My mother is Mother Nature
My father is the Lord of All
All the devotees are my relatives
The entire universe is my home.

I offer this (food) unto Om, that truth which is Brahman.

May the entire world be filled with peace and joy.

BIBLIOGRAPHY

We think you'll enjoy, as we have, the following books and publications.

Books

(All books listed are in paperback)

Abehsera, Michel, *Zen Macrobiotic Cooking*, Secaucus, N.J.: University Books, 1968. *An excellent introduction to macrobiotic cooking.*

Aihara, Cornellia, *The Chico-san Cookbook*, Chico, Calif.: Chico-san Inc., 1972. *A lot of good macrobiotic and tofu recipes.*

Airola, Paavo O., N.D., Ph.D., *Are You Confused?*, Phoenix, Ariz.: Health Plus, 1971. *A lot of valuable information in this book by one of the world's most reknowned naturopaths.*

Bethel, May, *The Healing Power of Herbs*, North Hollywood, Calif.: Wilshire Books Company, 1968. *If it's still in print, this inexpensive book is one of the best introductions to herbs that we know about. We have gotten a lot of value from it.*

Bragg, Paul C., N.D., Ph.D., *Toxicless Diet*, Desert Hot Springs, Calif.: Health Science, 1976. *This little booklet, which is one of a series, is must reading for anyone interested in a healthy diet.*

Brodsky, Greg, *From Eden to Aquarius—The Book of Natural Healing*, New York: Bantam, 1974. *An excellent book, with a great chapter: "Food as Natural Medicine."*

Brown, Edward Espe, *Tassajara Cooking*, Berkeley, Calif.: Shambhala, 1973. *The kind of cookbook we like . . . many recipes to create with. It was produced by the members of the Zen Center community in San Francisco. Beautiful illustrations by Del Calson.*

Dufty, William, *Sugar Blues*, New York, Warner Books, 1975. *This book should be required reading for every American. Read it and kick the sugar habit!*

Farm, The, *The Farm Vegetarian Cookbook*, Summertown, Tenn.: The Book Publishing Company, 1975. *An enjoyable, inexpensive book with recipes for soybeans, soymilk, tofu, tempeh, soy flour, gluten, etc.*

Farr, Barbara, *Super Soy*, New Canaan, Conn.: Keats, 1976. *A lot of good recipes in this well-designed book on the versatile soybean.*

176

Ford, Marjorie Winn, Susan Hillgard, and Mary Faulk Kooch, *The Deaf Smith Country Cookbook*, New York: Collier, 1973. *One of the better whole-foods cookbooks. A good buy.*

Goldbeck, Nikki and David, *The Super Market Handbook*, New American Library, New York: 1973. *As important to have in your home as a dictionary or encyclopedia. It directs you to all the best chemical-free foods that are available in the supermarket with brand recommendations. It also has excellent recipes.*

Gregory, Dick, *Cookin' with Mother Nature: Natural Diet for Folks Who Eat*, New York: Perennial Library, 1974. *One of our favorites. Especially since Dick entertains while he educates.*

Hewitt, Jean, *The New York Times Natural Foods Cookbook*, New York: Avon, 1972. *Over 700 recipes. One of the best natural foods cookbooks.*

Hurd, Frank J., D.C., and Rosalie Hurd, B.S., *Ten Talents Cookbook*, Chisholm, Minn.: Dr. and Mrs. Frank J. Hurd Publishers, 1968. *Don't be put off by the old-fashioned look of this book. It is filled with hundreds of good recipes and lots of valuable information.*

Kloss, Jethro, *Back to Eden*, Riverside, Calif.: Lifeline Books, 1972. *The bible of herbal remedies. No family or individual should be without one.*

Kulvinskas, Viktoras, M.S., *Survival into the 21st Century*, Wethersfield, Conn.: Omangod Press, 1975. *As the title suggests, a survival book for a new age. A comprehensive study of the many facets of natural healing and a helpful guide to nature's most beneficial foods.*

Kushi, Michio, *The Book of Macrobiotics*, Tokyo, Japan: Japan Publications, 1977. *The long awaited book about the theory and practice of macrobiotics by its foremost authority.*

Lappe, Frances Moore, *Diet for a Small Planet*, New York: Ballantine, 1971. *All about vegetarian protein sources with emphasis on combining foods for added protein value. Many good recipes.*

Larson, Gena, *Better Foods for Better Babies*, New Canaan, Conn.: Pivot Original Health Books, 1972. *An excellent little book from which we've picked up some healthful hints.*

Levy, Juliette De Bairacli, *Nature's Children*, New York: Warner Paperback Library, 1968. *A wonderful book about herbs. Read it whether you're raising children or not.*

Lust, John B., *About Raw Juices*, London: Thorson's Publishing, Ltd., 1962. *All about the nutritional and healing properties of raw juices.*

177

Lust, John B., *The Herb Book*, New York: Bantam, 1974. *A handy, comprehensive encyclopedia of herbs and herb remedies.*

Newman, Laura, *Make Your Juicer Your Drug Store*, New York: Benedict Lust Publications, 1970. *As the title suggests, raw juice therapy can save you a fortune in prescriptions.*

Ohsawa, Lima, *The Art of Just Cooking*, Brookline, Mass.: Autumn Press, 1974. *An excellent introduction to macrobiotic cooking, with excellent recipes.*

Ranill, June, *The El Molino Cookbook*, City of Industry, Calif.: El Molino Mills, 1976. *This inexpensive spiral-bound book is one of the best whole-foods cookbooks we've come across. An excellent introduction to whole foods with lots of easy-to-follow recipes.*

Rose, Ian F., *Faith, Love and Seaweed*, New York: Award, 1969. *Unfortunately this book is out of print. It is one of the finest books written on health food and the vegetarian diet; by the father of Murray Rose, the Olympic swimming champion, who was raised as a vegetarian.*

Shelton, Herbert M., *The Hygienic Care of Children*, Chicago, Ill.: Natural Hygiene Press, 1970. *A book that pulls no punches about the natural care of children. Every parent or expectant parent should read it.*

Shurtleff, William, and Akiko Aoyagi, *The Book of Tofu*, Kanagawa-Ken, Japan: Autumn Press, 1975. *An extraordinary book. Over 200 tofu recipes. With beautiful illustrations and a fascinating text.*

Shurtleff, William, and Akiko Aoyagi, *The Book of Miso*, Kanagawa-Ken, Japan: Autumn Press, 1976. *What Shurtleff and Aoyagi have done for tofu, they now do for miso in this excellent companion to* The Book of Tofu.

Walker, N.W., *Diet and Salad Suggestions*, Phoenix, Ariz.: Norwalk Press, 1940. *A very modest title for this giant of a book on health and nutrition.*

Walker, N.W., *Raw Vegetable Juices*, Phoenix, Arizona, Norwalk Press, 1936. *Another modest title for another giant of a book. Our favorite book of raw fruit and vegetable juices.*

Wiener, Joan, *Victory Through Vegetables*, New York: Holt, Rinehart and Winston, 1970. *A book that will get used often, as it is filled with many delightful recipes.*

178

Publications

The New Sun, 1520 East 10th Street, Brooklyn, N.Y. 11230.
New Age, 32 Station Street, Brookline, Mass. 02146.
Well-Being, 833 W. Fir, San Diego, Calif. 92101.
Alternatives, P. O. Box 330139, Miami, Florida 33133.
East West, 233 Harvard Street, Brookline, Mass. 02146.
Best ways, 466 Foothill Blvd., La Canada, Calif. 91011.
Let's Live, 444 North Larchmont Blvd., Los Angeles, Calif. 90004.
Life and Health, Review and Herald Publ., 6856 Eastern Ave., Wash. D.C. 20012.
The Herbalist, BiWorld Publ., 224 North Draper Lane, P. O. Box 62, Provo, Utah 84601.
Prevention, Rodale Press, 33 East Minor St., Emmaus, Pa. 18049.
The Vegetarian Times, Suite 1838, 101 Park Avenue, New York, N.Y. 10017.

INDEX

Aduki beans, 72
Agar-agar, fruit, 136
Airola, Dr. Paavo, 10
Alfalfa seeds, 7
All-blend oil, 7
Almond butter, 7
Almonds, 7, 113
Amino acids, 9
Apple betty, granola, 149
Apple butter, 137
Apricot butter, 137
Are You Confused? (Airola), 172
Arrowroot, 17
Arrowroot flour, 6
Asanas, 170
Avocado salad dressing, 112
Avocado split, 134
Avocado yogurt salad, dressing, 127

Back to Eden (Kloss), 162
Banana bread, 41
Banana split, 134
Bananas, 131, 159
Barley, 57-58
Bean loaf, 75
Bean soup, black, 74
Beanburgers, 78-81
Beans, 61-75
Book of Macrobiotics, The (Kushi), 84
Book of Tofu, The (Shurtleff and
    Aoyagi), 91, 98
Bran, 6
Bread, 33-44
  banana, 41
  carrot cornbread, 38
  early American cornbread, 39
  easy rye, 40
  honey whole wheat, 36-37
  pita, 43
  white, 33-35
Bread and Circus, 85
Bread sticks, whole wheat, 41
Breast feeding, 156-158

Brewer's yeast, 7
Broth, vegetable, 28
Brownies, carob, 151
Buckwheat groats, 6, 53
  see also Kasha
Bulghur wheat, 6, 58-59
Butter
  almond, 7
  apple, 137
  apricot, 137
  peanut, 7, 114
  safflower, 124
  sesame (tahini), 7, 105-106
Buttermilk, 123

Camomile tea, 7, 121
Candy, granola, 151
Carob, 147
Carrot cornbread, 38
Carrot juice, 140
Carrots, 13-14
Cashews, 7, 114-115
Casseroles
  Mediterranean soybean, 64
  millet, 52
  soybean, 65
Cheese, 122
Chia seed, 109
Chick-peas, 6, 67-68
  see also Garbanzos
Chili, vegetarian, 73
Chinese wok dinner, 20
Chocolate, 147
Cider, 143
Cigarette smoking, 154
Cleansing foods, 109, 121, 140, 153
Colas, 139-140
Cookies
  granola, 150
  sesame oatmeal, 148
Corn oil, 7
Cornbread
  carrot, 38
  early American, 39
Cornmeal, 6
Cous-cous, 6, 45-46

180

Crackerjacks, 150
Crackers, sesame whole wheat, 40
Curry, vegetable, 23
Dairy foods, 121-127
Date sugar, 7
Davis, Adelle, 33
Diet and Salad Suggestions (Walker), 117
Diet for a Small Planet (Lappe), 61
Disease, prevention of, 169-173
Doctors, opinion of, 172
Dressing, salad
  avocado, 112
  avocado yogurt, 127
  tahini, 106

East West Journal, The (magazine), 84, 172
Edison, Thomas, 172-173
Eggs, 6
Erewhon Store, 85
Exercise, 170-171

Farm Foods Tempeh Kit, 100-101
Felafel, 68
Fermented foods, 100
Flaxseed, 109
Flour, whole wheat, 6
Folk Medicine (Jarvis), 164
Foods, basic, 6-7
Foods and herbs, medicinal qualities of, 161-165
Fritini burgers, 80
Fructose, 7
Fruit, 129-137
  canned, 131
  citrus, 131
  dried and dehydrated, 131-132
  drinks, 132
  pudding, 136
  salad, 132
Fruit and dairy lunch, 135
Fruit and nut balls, 148

Gandhi, Mahatma, 47

Garbanzos, 6, 67-68
  see also Chick-peas
Gomasio, 107
  see also Sesame salt
Grains, whole, 33-59
Granola, 55-56
  baby's, 159
  bars, 149
  cookies, 150

Hamburgers, criticism of, 77-78
Health expositions, 172
Herbs, 161-165
Holistic health seminars, 172
Honey, 7
Hummus, 68

Ice cream sundae, tahini, 106
Ice pops, yogurt, 151
Illness, prevention of, 169-173
Indian vegetarian cookery, 23-24
Indian wok dinner, 20
Integral Yoga Hatha (Satchidananda), 170
Integral Yoga Institute, 36, 46, 170, 174
Integral Yoga Retreat, 174

Juices, 139-143

Kasha, 6, 53
  see also Buckwheat groats
Kelp, 7
Kinugoshi, 90, 98-99

Lacto-vegetarians, 121
La Leche League, 156
Learning Tree, The, 92
Lentil loaf, 71
Lentil millet patties, 81
Lentils, 6, 69-71
  curried with rice, 70
  salad, 71
  soup, 70
Liver, chopped vegetarian, 26

181

Macrobiotic diet system, 47
Macrobiotics, 83-87
Mantra, 171
Maple syrup, 7
Milk
  almond, 114
  cashew, 114, 115
  cow's, 121-122, 156
  goat's, 122
  human, 156-157
  soy, 66
  substitutes for babies, 157-158
Milkshake, banana cashew, 115
Millet, 6, 51-52
  baby's, 159
  casserole, 52
  and vegetables, 52
Miso, 7, 85
  soup, 86
  spread, 87
  yogurt dip, 127
Molasses, blackstrap, 7
Mother's milk supply, ways to increase, 155
Mu tea, 143
Muesli, 56
Muffins
  cornmeal and rye, 39
  yogurt bran, 38
Mung beans, 7
Mushroom barley soup, 58

Natural Diet for Folks That Eat: Cookin'
  with Mother Nature (Gregory),
  167-168
Naturopath, 172
Nerimiso, 87
New Age Journal, The (magazine), 172
New Sun, The (magazine), 172
Nituke vegetables, 21
Nuts, 113-115

Oatmeal, 54-57
  cinnamon-raisin, 54
  date blend, 54
  water, 155

Oats, 6
Olive oil, 7
Osahwa, Georges, 83

Pancakes, whole-grain, 42
Papaya split, 134
Peanut butter, 7, 114
Peanut oil, 7
Peanuts, 114
Peppermint tea, 7
Peppers, stuffed with cous-cous, 46
Pita bread, 43
Play dough, 34
Potato chips, 147
Prayers, 173-175
Pregnancy, 153-155
Prevention Magazine (June 1977), 101
Protein, 9-11
Protein powder, 7
Pudding, fruit, 136
Pumpkin seeds, 6, 108-109

Rainbow salad, 133
Raita, 126
Raw Vegetable Juices (Walker), 140
Rice, brown, 6, 47-51, 84
  basic, 48
  cream of, 50-51
  curried lentils with, 70
  fried with onions, 49
  pressure-cooked, 49
  soup, 50
  sweet, 49

Safflower oil, 7
Salads
  apple-jack, 125
  carrot and raisin, 29
  chick-pea, 65
  fruit, 132
  Greek, 30
  guacamole, 31
  lentil, 71
  rainbow, 133
  raw, 29-31
  soybean, 65

182

spinach with sesame seed dressing, 30
sprout, 112
tahini dressing, 106
tofu, 97
Salt
kelp, 107
sesame, 107
Sandwich
open-face avocado cheese, 125
tofu, 97
Satchidananda Ashram, 174
Satchidananda, Swami, 154, 169
Sauces, 117-119
blueberry, 133
ginger tamari, 118
onion tahini, 119
tahini, 105, 119
whole wheat, 118
yogurt blue cheese, 127
Scones, whole wheat, 43
Sea salt, 7
Seeds, 103-112
Sesame butter, *see* Tahini
Sesame oil, 7
Sesame salt, 107
see also Gomasio
Sesame seeds, 6, 104-106
Sesame soy milk, 66
Shaklee, 7
Sherbert, yogurt, 151
Shoyu, 84-85
Snacks, 145-150
Soda pop, 139-141
Soup
aduki bean, 72
black bean, 74
Dr. D'Adamo's, 27
lentil, 70
miso, 86
vegetable, 27
Soy milk, 66
Soybeans, 6, 62-65
casserole, 64, 65
salad, 65
soy milk, 66

roasted, 67
Soyburgers, 80
Soyflower, 6
Spaghetti, 117
Spike (vegetable) salt, 7
Spreads, bread
sweet cheese, 125
tahini, 106
Sprouting, 110-111
Sprouts, 110-112
Squash, honey, 26
Sugar, 147
Sunflower oil, 7
Sunflower seeds, 6, 108, 109
Supermarket Handbook, The
(Goldbeck), 122

Taboulleh, 59
Tahini, 7, 105-106
Tahini candy roll, 147
Tamari, 84-85
Tamari sauce, 7
Tea
apple spearmint, 142
camomile, 7
for colds and flu, 164
for colic and teething, 164
for coughs, 164
for fever, 162-163
for headache, 163
for morning sickness, 155
Mu, 143
for nerves, 165
for pain, 165
peppermint, 7
to promote easy childbirth, 155
for sinus congestion, 165
for sore throat, 164
for stomachache, 165
Three-grain breakfast cereal, 57
Toast, herb, 37
Tofu, 62, 89-101
homemade, 92-96
recipes, 97-98
Tomatoes, 117
Tempeh, 100-101

183

Tempura vegetables, 21-22

Upma, 24
Utensils, types needed, 5

Vegetables, 13-31
  casseroles, 25-26
  cooking, 16-26
  and millet, 52
  selecting, 14-15
Vegetarianism, reasons for, 2-3

Waffles, 43
Water, spring, 141
Weaning, 158-159
Well-Being (magazine), 172
Wheat germ, 6
Whole grains, storage of, 59
Wok cookery, 17-21

Yin and Yang, 83-84
Yoga, 170-171
Yogi's lunch, 135
Yogurt, 123-127
  ice pops, 151
  sherbert, 151
  sprout salad in, 113
  tahini, 105

Zen Macrobiotics, 83

PHOTO CREDITS

Andrew Unangst
The Zurbel Family, facing Introduction page
Wok, 18
Prescription Lemon, 160
Waxburger, 166

Ava Grodner and Carlo Annese
Kitchen Soldier, 4
Cooking Couple, 12
Steamer Basket, 16
Jonathan Playing with Beans, 60
Oliver Acknowledges the East, 82
Tofu Kit, 88
Hand Holding Sprouts, 102
Sprouting Jar, 110

Victor Pilosof
Jonathan Juicing, 138

Victor Zurbel
Swamiji and Oliver, Dedication page
Boys on Elephant, 8
Oliver Eating Knackebrod, 32
Knackebrod, 44
Food for Thought, 76
Sauce , 116
Oliver Says "Cheese," 120
Reclining with Grapes, 128
Snacking on Rice Cakes, 144
Mother and Child, 152